Chris Cleary, Bill Holden, Terry Cooney **ABAX Ltd.**

TOP-UP
Listening

Series Editor: Maurice Jamall

3

ABAX

Series Editor: Maurice Jamall
Project Manager: Alastair Graham-Marr
Syllabus Design: Maurice Jamall / Alastair Graham-Marr

Editing and Proofing:
Maurice Jamall
Alastair Graham-Marr
Hugh Graham-Marr

Lexical Analysis: Rob Waring
Interactive Word List devised by Maurice Jamall
Compilation of Word Lists: Hugh Graham-Marr

Published by ABAX Ltd.,
Tokyo and San Francisco

Editorial Office • Tel: +81(0)-44-813-2909 / Fax +81(0)-44-813-2916

email • sales@abax.net

homepage • www.abax.net

Layout and Cover Design by Design Office TERRA
Illustrations by Glen Giron, Alfred Rosales and Leo Gultura of
Raketshop, Philippines.
Many thanks to Tina Ferrato, Guy Modica and David Moran for
help in checking the scripts.

Large print version ©2007 ABAX Ltd. Printed in Singapore
ISBN 978-1-896942-15-5

Inside *Top-Up Listening*

Top-Up Listening is a three-book skills-based series designed to help elementary to low-intermediate level students of English improve their listening abilities. The series gives students the chance to hear English as it is naturally used, in a wide variety of contexts including formal and informal conversations, announcements, telephone talk, and much, much more. In other words, *Top-Up Listening* provides students with the opportunity to develop their listening skills in the wide range of situations that they may well meet in the real world.

Organization

Each book in the *Top-Up Listening* series consists of 15 units built around topics and themes selected for their appropriacy to teenagers and young adults. Each unit is designed to take between 50 and 70 classroom minutes. At the back of the book students are provided with the scripts of the listening tasks and a glossary* of useful words and expressions. There is also space for students to include words they choose themselves.

Listening Task Types

The listening activities in *Top-Up Listening* are designed to develop different kinds of skills including listening for main points, for general understanding, for specific information and inferencing. Each unit has a main listening task which forms the basis of the unit. Some listenings are longer and introduce students to extensive listening. Other listenings are shorter and develop students' intensive listening abilities. The language in the listenings is graded to meet the level of the students, but naturally occurring features of spoken English are retained to give students listening material which realistically simulates authentic speech and is at the same time challenging but within reach. An American English model is used but other forms of native-speaker English have also been included to introduce and expose students to the different types of English they will encounter outside the classroom.

Listening Clinic

A key focus in *Top-Up Listening* is the *Listening Clinics*. These are short, intensive listening tasks which highlight high-frequency phonological points. Students' difficulties understanding spoken English often come from an inability to decode a stream of connected speech. In each *Listening Clinic*, students focus on a single aspect of pronunciation.** Focusing intensively on these high-frequency features helps students grow more comfortable with English as it is spoken in the real world.

* The glossary is interactive requiring students to provide their own definitions or translations as well as locate items from definitions. By doing this students consolidate and review their work more thoroughly.

** This includes weak forms, assimilation, liaison and intonation and its uses. We have devised a set of terms to describe phonology which demystifies and simplifies so that the students are not put off by technical jargon.

Understanding Spoken English

Spoken English is very different from written English. When words are written down, there are spaces between them showing where one ends and the next word begins. For example, we write: "Would you like a sandwich?" But when we speak, there are no clear spaces, so we say:

"wouldyoulikeasandwich?"

To make things more difficult, sounds in words often mix or are lost, and so we say:

"wujewlaikasanwich?"

Top-Up Listening explains how English is spoken in the sections called *Listening Clinics*. Here you learn how to recognize the way people speak English and use this information to help you better understand what is being said and get to the speaker's meaning quicker. Here are some of the key points covered in the *Listening Clinics*:

1. Lost Sounds: In naturally spoken English, sounds are sometimes lost altogether.
   Example: *He's a postman.* The *t* sound is lost, so we hear: *He's a posman.*

2. Joined Sounds: When words end with a consonant and the following word begins with a vowel, the consonant 'jumps over' so that speech is smooth:
   Example: *He's an artist.* When spoken, it sounds like: *He sa nartist.*

3. Helping Sounds: When two vowels are next to each other, a "helping sound" often comes between them to make speaking easier. There are three helping sounds: *y*, *w*, and *r*.
   Examples: *y*: *She isn't here.* This becomes: *She-y-isn't here.*
            w: *I'd like to open the window.* This becomes: *I'd like to-w-open...*
            r: *America and Canada.* this becomes: *America-r-and Canada.*

4. Changing Sounds: Sounds can change from the spelling in spoken English.
   Examples: *He lives in Belgium.* The *n* becomes an *m* sound, so what you hear is: *He lives im Belgium.*
            I like football. The *b* changes to a *p* (the *t* is lost), and so what you hear is: *I like foopall.*

5. Weak Forms: The schwa (the upside-down *e* in the pronunciation alphabet) is the most common sound in English. Vowels are often spoken weakly. Say *Canada* and then say *Japan*. The first *a* sound in each country is different. In Canada the first *a* is strong and in Japan it is weak.

We hope you find using *Top-Up Listening* to be an enjoyable and rewarding experience.

In Your Own Time

Each unit in this textbook ends with a section called *In Your Own Time*. Here we ask you to work alone after the lesson so that you can review the things you did in class. If you spend some time each week reviewing what you study in class, you will make faster progress with your English.

At the back of your textbook, you will find the following:

- the scripts for all the listening exercises (pages 79 to 93).
- word lists with words and expressions from each unit (pages 94 to 102).
- your own copy of the CD that your teacher uses in the class.

Look at the back of the book now. Find the word lists, scripts and your CD.

Here are a few ways to use your textbook on your own:

Build Your Vocabulary

In each unit, you will see new words. In the word list you will find nine words and definitions. Some of the information is missing. You can complete the missing information by going through the unit again and reading through the scripts. If you want to, use a bilingual dictionary. If it helps you remember the word, write a translation in your own language. There is also space at the end of the word list for you to choose three new words for yourself. Try to choose words which you think are especially useful. Perhaps during the lesson, the teacher taught you some extra words and expressions not in the textbook. If you want to, you could write some of those words here. Don't add too many new words though. A good rule is to try to learn between eight and twelve new words per unit.

Work On Your Listening

During the lesson, your teacher has to teach the class at a speed that is comfortable for the most students. Sometimes the lessons may be too fast for you. Sometimes the lesson may go too slowly. But when you use your CD at home, you can always go at just the right speed for you. Here are some ways to make the most of your textbook to improve your listening:

- look at your answers to the listening tasks and listen to the recordings again.
- read through the scripts and check any new words and expressions, then close your book and listen to the recording(s) once more.
- read the script and listen to the CD at the same time.
- listen to the two *Listening Clinics* and then read them aloud.

One last piece of advice: don't do too much at one time. A good rule is *a little and often*. Just as we eat three times a day, it is much better to study for 15 or 20 minutes every day rather than for a long time just once a week.

By making the most of your textbook, you will really start to make progress with your English. Good luck with your studies.

Top-Up 3 Contents

Good to see you again

⊹Let's Start!

Work with your partner. Draw lines to match each first name on the left with its short form on the right. The first one is done for you.

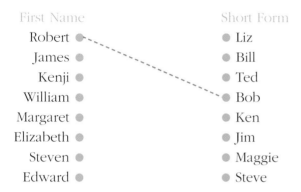

First Name	Short Form
Robert	Liz
James	Bill
Kenji	Ted
William	Bob
Margaret	Ken
Elizabeth	Jim
Steven	Maggie
Edward	Steve

Do you use short forms for names in your country?
Who do you usually use them with?

⊹Before You Listen

Work with your partner. Look at the greetings in Column A. Place a check (✓) next to the ones we use when we meet someone for the first time. Put a circle (◯) next to the ones we usually use when we talk to people we already know.

	A			B
....	How've you been?	●	●	Good, thanks. And you?
....	How are you doing?	●	●	You too.
....	How do you do?	●	●	Okay.
....	Pleased to meet you.	●	●	Oh, nothing much.
....	Good to see you again.	●	●	How do you do?
....	What's new?	●	●	It's nice to meet you too.
....	Please call me (Mike).	●		
....	How's things?	●		

Now look at the replies in Column B. Draw lines to match each greeting with a suitable reply. Some replies can be used more than once.

Compare your answers with another pair.

Listen to four conversations. Look at the pictures. Write the number of the conversation under the correct picture. There is one picture too many.

Conversation .....

Conversation .....

Conversation .....

Conversation .....

Conversation .....

Check your answers with your partner.

Listen to Conversation 4 again. Draw lines to match the people in Column A with the information about them in Column B.

A	B
Ken and Mark ●	● are meeting for the first time
Steve and Ken ●	● are students
Mark and Steve ●	● are brothers
Ken, Mark and Steve ●	● have met before

Check your answers with your partner.

Sometimes speakers say vowels weakly.

Example	Good to see you again. → Good tø see yøy again.

Listen to the dialogue. Draw lines through vowels which are spoken *weakly*.

A: What do you do for a living?
B: I'm a teacher.
A: Really? Where?
B: At a junior high school in Tokyo.
A: Do you like it?
B: Yeah. It's an interesting job.

Check your answers with your partner. Now say the dialogue together.

Practice!

Work as a class. Practice greeting each other. Use the expressions to help you. Move around, and talk to a few of your classmates. Try to use different expressions each time.

Greetings

- Hello (Name).
- Hi (Name).
- Good to see you.
- It's been a while.
- How are you?
- Haven't seen you for ages.

Replies

- Great (thanks).
- Good (thanks).
- Fine (thanks).
- Pretty good (thanks).
- Not so bad.
- Can't complain.

Questions

- How have you been?
- How's it going?
- How are things?

Return Questions

- How about you?
- What about you?
- And you?
- How're things with you?

Now work with a partner. Ask and answer the questions.

- How many people did you talk to?
- Can you remember their names?
- What did you talk about?

Listen to the conversations again. Circle *P* if the meeting was planned. Circle *C* if the meeting happened by chance.

Conversation 1	P	C
Conversation 2	P	C
Conversation 3	P	C
Conversation 4	P	C

:Listening Clinic Two: Joined Sounds

CD Track: 6

When a word ends in a consonant sound and the next word starts with a vowel, the two sounds join.

Example	Consonants and vowels often link in spoken English. →
	Consonant sand vowel soften lin kin spoke nEnglish.

Work with your partner. Look at the sentences. Circle places where sounds may *join*. The first one is done for you.

1. What's up Alan? You look a bit pale.
2. I haven't seen you for ages.
3. I've been out of town for two weeks.
4. I'm enjoying my new job very much.
5. He's an interesting guy.
6. Mike just got a new job in Tokyo.

Listen and check. Now say the sentences.

▶Try It Out!

Work with your partner. Use the information and roleplay the situation.

Student A

Your neighbor, (Student B) has just returned from vacation. Ask about his/her holiday. Follow the prompts and have a conversation.

Student B

You have just returned from a two-week vacation. Talk to your neighbor, (Student A). Tell him/her about your holiday.

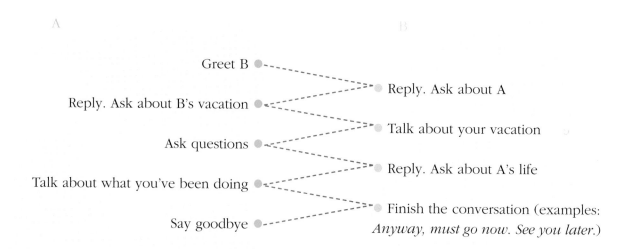

A
B

Greet B ●- - - - -
                              ●→ Reply. Ask about A
Reply. Ask about B's vacation ●←
                              ●→ Talk about your vacation
Ask questions ●←
                              ●→ Reply. Ask about A's life
Talk about what you've been doing ●←
                              ●→ Finish the conversation (examples:
Say goodbye ●- - - - -   *Anyway, must go now. See you later.*)

▶In Your Own Time

Turn to page 102 and complete the word list. Use your dictionary if you want to. Use the CD at the back of your book and listen to the recordings in this unit again. The script for this unit is on pages 79 and 80.

Unit 2 I've lost my rucksack

⊳Let's Start!

Work on your own. Check (✓) your answers to the quiz.

- How would you feel if you suddenly noticed your bag was missing?
  ☐ angry   ☐ scared   ☐ worried   ☐ foolish

- What would you do first if you noticed your bag was missing?
  ☐ go back to where you last had it for sure
  ☐ ask people near you if they took it
  ☐ contact the police
  ☐ swear

- Where do people usually lose things? Choose two.
  ☐ at the airport   ☐ in a store   ☐ on the train   ☐ in a taxi

- What would you do if you found a bag on the street?
  ☐ keep it   ☐ open it   ☐ leave it alone   ☐ give it to a police officer

Compare your answers with your partner.

⊳Words

Work with your partner. Put the words from the box into the two categories. The first one is done for you.

Materials	Features
	logo

logo	plastic	leather	strap	buckle
handle	canvas	wheels	rubber	nylon

Work on your own. Check (✓) *Yes* or *No* to answer the question.

Do you own the following things?

	Yes	No
• a leather briefcase	☐	☐
• a belt with a large, silver buckle	☐	☐
• a suitcase with wheels	☐	☐
• a wallet or purse with a logo	☐	☐
• a handbag with a wooden handle	☐	☐
• a plastic umbrella	☐	☐
• a canvas rucksack	☐	☐
• a sportsbag with long straps	☐	☐
• a nylon money belt	☐	☐

Compare your answers with your partner.

Which two things in the list would you most like to buy? Which thing(s) would you never buy?

:Let's Listen!   CD Tracks: 7, 8, 9, 10

Listen to four conversations. Draw lines to match each conversation with the lost item. Then draw lines to match each lost item with the place where it was lost.

	Lost Item		Place
	• a suitcase •		• a railway station
Conversation 1 •	• a rucksack •		• an airport
Conversation 2 •	• a handbag •		• a bus depot
Conversation 3 •	• a shopping bag •		• on a bus
Conversation 4 •	• a sports bag •		• in a restaurant
	• a money belt •		• a tennis court
	• a briefcase •		

Check your answers with your partner.

:Listen Again   CD Tracks: 7, 8, 9, 10

Listen to the conversations again. Complete the chart with information about each lost item.

	Size	Color	Material	Feature(s)
Conversation 1				large silver buckle, short handstrap
Conversation 2		brown		
Conversation 3	big			
Conversation 4			hard shell	

Check your answers with your partner.

When a speaker wants to show that information is new, s/he puts stress on the word which has the new information.

Example	A: Have you seen my <u>hat</u>? B: Which <u>one</u>? A: The <u>blue</u> hat. The hat with <u>stripes</u>.

Listen to the dialogue. Underline the words where the speaker puts stress to *show new information*. The first two are done for you.

A: Oh no! I can't find my <u>wallet</u>.

B: Is <u>this</u> it?

A: No. Mine's a brown wallet. Brown with a logo.

B: What kind of logo?

A: A bull. A bull with horns.

B: Ah! Here it is.

Check your answers with your partner. Now say the dialogue together.

⊡Practice!

Work with your partner. Look at the pictures.

Student A: You have lost some of the items. Describe the things you lost.

Student B: You are the clerk at the *Lost and Found*. Try to find the missing items. Use the model dialogue on the following page to help you. Choose your own words where the _____ is. Take turns to be the *Lost and Found* clerk.

A: Excuse me?

B: Yes _____ . How can I help you?

A: I've lost my _____ .

B: I see _____ . And what does it look like?

A: Well it's _____ , and it has _____ and a _____ .

B: Is this your _____ ?

A: [if B is right] Yes, that's it.

　　[if B is wrong] No, that's not mine.

Now Listen Back

CD Tracks: 7, 8, 9, 10

Listen to the conversations again. Circle *Yes* if the missing item has been found. Circle *No* if it has not.

Conversation 1	Yes	No
Conversation 2	Yes	No
Conversation 3	Yes	No
Conversation 4	Yes	No

Check your answers with your partner.

Listening Clinic Two: Stressing New Information

CD Track: 12

Work with your partner. Look at the sentences. Underline the words which the speaker may stress to *show new information*.

1. Did you say you lost a *Gucci* purse or was it a *Fendi*?
2. I bought a cheap briefcase, not an expensive one.
3. Have you seen my yellow shopping bag? It was near the black one.
4. I don't like those nylon wallets, but the leather wallets are nice.
5. Yes sir, but what kind of briefcase did you lose?
6. I left it on the morning bus, not the afternoon one.

Listen and check. Now say the sentences.

▶Try It Out!

Work on your own. You are in a department store and you have lost your bag. Use your imagination and complete the chart with information to describe your bag.

Color: ....

Size: ....

Features: ....

Maker: ....

Contents: ....

Where you lost it: ....

Work with your partner and roleplay a conversation between the *Lost and Found* clerk and the shopper. Describe your bag. Has it been found? Take turns.

▶In Your Own Time

Turn to pages 102 and 103 and complete the word list. Use your dictionary if you want to. Use the CD at the back of your book and listen to the recordings in this unit again. The script for this unit is on pages 80, 81 and 82.

I'd like you to meet my brother

▸Let's Start!

Work with your partner. Place a check (✓) in the boxes to show what kind of person uses each title.

	Mr.	Miss	Mrs.	Ms.
A married man	☐	☐	☐	☐
An unmarried man	☐	☐	☐	☐
A married woman	☐	☐	☐	☐
An unmarried woman	☐	☐	☐	☐

Can you think of any other titles used in English?

▸Before You Listen

Work with your partner. Number the greetings in order from *1* (most formal) to *4* (least formal).

.... Mr. Harris, I'd like you to meet my wife, Jane.
.... Martin, this is my wife, Jane.
.... Mr. Harris, allow me to introduce my wife, Jane.
.... Marty, say "Hi" to Jane.

Now draw lines to match each greeting with a suitable reply.

Mr. Harris, I'd like you to meet my wife, Jane. ● ● Hi, Jane.
Martin, this is my wife, Jane. ● ● It's a pleasure to meet you, Mrs. Cooper.
Mr. Harris, allow me to introduce my wife, Jane. ● ● Nice to meet you, Jane.
Marty, say "Hi" to Jane. ● ● Pleased to meet you, Mrs. Cooper.

Check your answers with another pair.

Listen to four conversations. Write the number of the conversation under the picture.

Conversation .....

Conversation .....

Conversation .....

Conversation .....

Check your answers with your partner.

▶Listen Again CD Track: 16

Listen to Conversation 4 again. Place a check (✓) for *Yes*, or a cross (✗) for *No* to answer the question.

Have the people met before?

	Kathy	John	John's parents
Mr. Burns	☐	☐	☐
Mrs. Burns	☐	☐	☐

▶Listening Clinic One: Mixed Sounds

Sometimes when two consonant sounds come together, one at the end of one word and one at the beginning of the next, they mix and make a new sound.

Examples	Third year →Thir jear
	In Britain →Im Britain
	Could you →coujew

Listen to the dialogue. Circle the places where you hear *mixed sounds*.

A: Hey Leslie. Do you know who that girl is over there?

B: You mean the pretty girl dressed in black? That's Annie.

A: She's gorgeous. I want you to introduce me to her.

B: Sure. But I should let you know—she's already got a boyfriend.

Check your answers with your partner. Now say the dialogue together.

▶Practice!

Work in a group of three.

Student A: You know both Student B and Student C.

Student B: You know Student A but not Student C.

Student C: You know Student A but not Student B.

Student A: Introduce the other two people to each other. Say something about the people. Use the information below if you want to or use your own ideas.

Students B and C: Have a short conversation together.

Names		Relationships	Interesting Facts
Alex	Sarah	a friend from school	she just moved here
Kenji	Naoko	a neighbor	she's visiting for the summer
David	Penny	a cousin	she's in the swim team with you
Philippe	Marie	a brother/sister	her mother is the Principal's assistant
Dan	Liz	an old teacher	she used to live in California

Take turns to be Student A.

▶Now Listen Back

Listen to the conversations again. Look at the statements. Circle the number of the conversation if the statement applies.

Statement	Conversation			
All speakers like each other.	1	2	3	4
The conversation is unwelcome.	1	2	3	4
The conversation is formal.	1	2	3	4
The conversation is informal.	1	2	3	4

⤷Listening Clinic Two: Mixed Sounds

Work with your partner. Look at the sentences. Circle places where sounds may *mix*.

1. I come from a very big family. I have seven brothers and sisters.
2. I think you know most of the people here, don't you?
3. This is my son, Brian. He'll be working with me this summer.
4. Ellen's new here. Would you show her around?
5. Hi. I don't think we've met yet. I'm Larry.
6. I'm sorry, I didn't catch your family name. Could you say it again?

Listen and check. Now say the sentences.

⤷Try It Out!

Part 1: Get Ready

Work on your own. You are at Alex's party. Use your imagination. Complete the information with your own ideas and make a "new" person.

Rolecard

Name: ....

Age: ....

Job: ....

Interests: ....

You know Alex because:

....

Part 2: Roleplay

Roleplay the party with your classmates.
Introduce yourself to the other guests. When you can, introduce people to each other.

⤷In Your Own Time

Turn to page 103 and complete the word list. Use your dictionary if you want to.
Use the CD at the back of your book and listen to the recordings in this unit again. The script for this unit is on pages 82, 83 and 84.

Final Call for Flight EA42

Let's Start!

Work with your partner. Look at the announcements. Draw lines from the announcement on the left to the place you hear it on the right.

| The 14:37 bound for St Louis is departing from Track 16. | ● airport |

| Will Passenger Bailey flying to Hong Kong contact the South Pacific Airlines information desk in Terminal Two, please? | ● hotel |

| The shuttle bus to Heathrow Airport will leave in five minutes. Thank you. | ● movie theater |

| We would like to remind patrons to turn off cell phones and pagers during the show. Thank you. | ● railway station |

What other kinds of announcements do you hear in hotels, railway stations, movie theaters and airports?

Before You Listen

Work with your partner. Look at the list of things you need to do when you take an international flight. Number the steps from *1* to *8* in the order you do them. The first one is done for you.

.... Get off the plane
__1__ Go into the arrivals hall
.... Get to the airport
.... Go to the check-in counter and get your boarding pass
.... Go to the baggage claim and collect your luggage
.... Go to the boarding gate
.... Get on the plane
.... Go through Customs and Immigration

Which step are the people in the pictures taking? Choose from the list.

....

....

....

....

▶ Let's Listen!

CD Tracks: 19, 20, 21, 22

Listen to four airport announcements. Draw lines to match the number of the announcement to the correct summary.

Announcement 1 ●

Announcement 2 ●

Announcement 3 ●

Announcement 4 ●

● Don't leave your bags alone

● Time to go

● We've found your daughter

● We're sorry to have kept you waiting

● Big bargains at Duty Free

● Someone's waiting for you

Check your answers with your partner.

▶ Listen Again

CD Tracks: 19, 20, 21, 22

Listen to the announcements again. Draw lines to join the announcement number to the person or people it is for and the purpose of the announcement.

	Person/People		Purpose of Announcement
Announcement 1 ●	● Mr. Singh	●	● don't leave your bags unattended
Announcement 2 ●	● passengers to Las Vegas	●	● go to the East Asian Airways lounge
Announcement 3 ●	● passengers to Hong Kong ●		● flight delayed but now boarding
Announcement 4 ●	● all passengers	●	● now boarding

In natural speech, sounds in words can change from the spelling. This often happens with the /t/ sound.

Example | LA to New York is a pre**tt**y busy route. → LA to New York is a pre**d**y busy route.
(the /t/ sound in *pretty* becomes a /d/)

Listen to the announcement. Circle places where sounds *change*.

Ladies and gentlemen, welcome aboard Flight 830 to Chicago via Portland. We'll be a little late taking off because of bad weather in Chicago. The flight should be pretty smooth most of the way but a storm is moving in our direction, so please keep your seatbelts fastened. We'll be stopping briefly in Portland before arriving in Chicago.

Check your answers with your partner. Now say the announcement.

Practice!

Work with your partner. Number the sentences from *1* to *4* to make two airport announcements. Take turns and practice reading each announcement aloud.

Announcement 1

.... We would like to apologize for the delayed departure.
.... The new departure time for this flight is 9:45.
.... This is due to heavy snow in Seattle.
.... Attention please, all passengers on Global Airlines Flight 873 to Seattle.

Announcement 2

.... We will begin boarding with business class passengers and passengers with young children.
.... Northern Airlines Flight 94 is now ready for boarding at Gate 11.
.... Please have your passports and boarding cards ready.
.... All other passengers are requested to remain seated until the next announcement.

Listen to the announcements again. Check (✓) what you should do in each situation.

Announcement 1

You are traveling on Flight NA115 to Las Vegas. What should you do?

☐ be ready to board the plane at 11:15 a.m.
☐ be ready to board the plane at 11:45 a.m.

Announcement 2

You are waiting for your flight and you need to go to the restroom. You are traveling alone and you have a large shoulder bag. What should you do?

☐ leave your bag on your seat so other passengers will know the seat is taken
☐ take your bag with you to the restroom

Announcement 3

Your name is Singh, and you are traveling on East Asian Airways Flight 28 to Honolulu. What should you do?

☐ go to the Jasmine Lounge
☐ nothing

Announcement 4

You are travelling alone in economy class on Flight 4, and your seat number is 36B. What should you do?

☐ get in line to board the plane
☐ wait for the next announcement

Check your answers with your partner.

Listening Clinic One: Changing Sounds — CD Track: 24

Work with your partner. Look at the sentences. Circle places where sounds may *change*.

1. Please go to the East Asian Airways lounge.
2. We'll be arriving in Boston at 15:30.
3. A lot of people are afraid of flying.
4. Put all metal objects into the tray, please.
5. The washrooms are out of order.
6. We're ready to begin boarding, ladies and gentlemen.

Listen and check. Now say the sentences.

▶Try It Out!

Work with your partner. Write an announcement for each piece of information. Take turns and practice reading your announcements aloud.

- North American Airlines NA281 to London / new departure time 11:45 / late arrival of connecting flight

- Passenger Lee / SK224 to Seoul / go to South Korean Airlines customer service desk (international departure lounge)

- Final call / California Airlines CA161 to San Francisco / Gate 23 (immediately)

....

....

....

....

....

▶In Your Own Time

Turn to pages 103 and 104 and complete the word list. Use your dictionary if you want to. Use the CD at the back of your book and listen to the recordings in this unit again. The script for this unit is on page 84.

Unit 5 — It's a great deal!

▶Let's Start!

Work with your partner. Look at the pictures advertising a holiday resort, a computer and a pair of shoes.

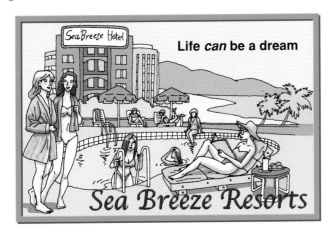

Choose three words from the box to describe each item.
Add one more word of your own to each list.

Resort	Shoes	Computer
....	....	....
....	....	....
....	....	....
....	....	....

■ fast   ■ powerful   ■ stylish   ■ scenic   ■ comfortable
■ peaceful   ■ soft   ■ easy to use   ■ relaxing

Compare your answers with another pair.
Do you want to buy either of the products? Do you want to visit the resort? Why (not)?

⁞▸Before You Listen

Work with your partner. Next to each adjective on the left, write two *strong* adjectives from the box which have similar meanings.

good ....

big ....

tasty ....

interesting ....

good-looking ....

surprising ....

▪ unbelievable	▪ fantastic	▪ huge	▪ stunning
▪ enormous	▪ gorgeous	▪ delicious	▪ superb
▪ spell-binding	▪ mouth-watering	▪ fascinating	▪ amazing

⁞▸Let's Listen!

CD Tracks: 25, 26, 27, 28

Listen to four commercials. Write the number of the commercial next to the product or service that is being advertised.

.... a movie .... an Internet service provider (ISP)

.... a CD .... a computer

.... a weight-loss product .... a car dealer

Check your answers with your partner.

⁞▸Listen Again

CD Track: 28

Listen to Commercial 4 again. Place a check (✓) to show the advantages of using Cosmo Cable.

☐ The Internet connection is always on.

☐ Cosmo Cable will give you a free computer if you sign up.

☐ It's much faster than a dial-up Internet service provider.

☐ You can have a one-month free trial.

☐ You don't have to pay any telephone charges.

☐ You will receive some free software.

☐ You can get free installation if you sign up this month.

Check your answers with your partner.

Speakers put strong stress on words in the sentence which are most important.

> **Example** : The <u>scenery</u> was absolutely <u>wonderful</u>.

Listen to the dialogue. Underline the words in each sentence that are most *strongly* stressed.

A: So how was your vacation at Club Tropicana?

B: It was really amazing. The weather was absolutely brilliant, the food was delicious and the staff were so friendly.

A: Sounds like you had a great time.

B: I did. But hey, everyone has a great time at Club Tropicana.

Check your answers with your partner. Now say the dialogue together.

Practice!

Work with your partner.

Student A: You are a sales clerk for *Big Cable*. Use the information in the table. Explain why *Big Cable* gives better service.

Student B: You are a customer who is currently using *Ace Online*. You are not happy with the service and are thinking about changing to *Big Cable*.

	Ace Online	Big Cable
Internet connection type	Dial-up modem	Cable modem (always on)
Connection speed	56 kilobytes per second	1.5 megabytes per second (about 30 times faster)
Monthly cost	$45	$39.95
Space for webpage	5 megabytes	15 megabytes
Technical support (telephone)	Mon-Fri 9-5	24 hrs/day, 365 days/year

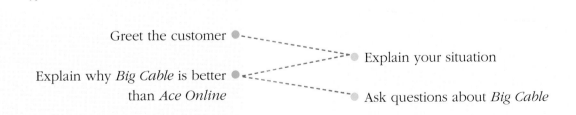

A

Greet the customer

Explain why *Big Cable* is better than *Ace Online*

B

Explain your situation

Ask questions about *Big Cable*

Listen to the commercials again. Place a check (✓) to show how the customer can buy or get more information about each product or service.

	Phone	Internet	Visit
Commercial 1	☐	☐	☐
Commercial 2	☐	☐	☐
Commercial 3	☐	☐	☐
Commercial 4	☐	☐	☐

Check your answers with your partner.

Listening Clinic Two: Stress In Sentences

CD Track: 30

Work with your partner. Look at the sentences. Underline the words which may be *strongly stressed*.

1. It's a really amazing album.
2. He's an absolutely brilliant guitarist.
3. This camera is incredibly cheap.
4. The Cortina is a lot faster than the Allegro.
5. It's the most exciting movie of the year.
6. This is a much better deal.

Listen and check. Now say the sentences.

▶Try It Out!

Work with your partner.

Student A

You are a sales clerk. Your want to sell one of
your possessions (your watch, cell phone, jacket,
pen, etc...) to your partner. Think of some good
sales points (design, features or functions, cost,
and so on). Whenyou are ready, begin your
sales talk.

You can start like this:
"Would you like to buy this ⬚⬚⬚⬚ ?
It's really ⬚⬚⬚⬚ ."

Student B

You are a customer. Listen to Student A's sales talk. Ask questions. If you think it's a good deal, agree
to buy. If not, refuse. You can try to get a better price!

Now change roles.

▶In Your Own Time

Turn to page 104 and complete the word list. Use your dictionary if you want to.
Use the CD at the back of your book and listen to the recordings in this unit again. The script
for this unit is on pages 85 and 86.

Unit 6 — That's not good enough

⊳Let's Start!

Work on your own. Check (✓) your answers to the quiz. What would you do in each situation?

- ▪ You are in a diner. You order a hot dog, with onions and tomato ketchup. The waiter brings you a hot dog with ketchup and mustard, but without onions. Do you...
  - ☐ call the waiter and point out his mistake?
  - ☐ eat the hot dog anyway?
  - ☐ not eat the hot dog but say nothing?

- ▪ You are in the non-smoking area of a restaurant. Two people at a nearby table start smoking. Do you...
  - ☐ go over and ask them not to smoke?
  - ☐ call the waiter and ask him to talk to the people?
  - ☐ stay quiet and do nothing?

- ▪ You order a pizza over the phone. You are told that pizza will be delivered in half an hour. One hour later the pizza still hasn't arrived. Do you...
  - ☐ phone and cancel the order?
  - ☐ phone and ask them to hurry up?
  - ☐ keep waiting and hope the pizza will arrive soon?

- ▪ You are in a movie theater. The two people in front of you have been talking non-stop since the movie started. Do you...
  - ☐ ask them politely but firmly to stop talking during the movie?
  - ☐ move to another seat where you can't hear them?
  - ☐ do nothing and hope someone else will tell them to be quiet?

- You are taking a taxi home from your local station. It usually takes about five minutes and costs five dollars. This taxi takes a different route. It takes ten minutes and costs more than ten dollars. Do you…
  - ☐ tell the taxi driver that you know he has tried to cheat you, and refuse to pay more than five dollars?
  - ☐ pay the ten dollars, but report him to the taxi company?
  - ☐ pay the ten dollars and do nothing?

Compare your answers with a partner.

Look at the four pictures. Match each to one question.

Have you ever experienced any of the situations from the quiz? If *yes*, what did you do? Have you ever complained about service you received? What happened?

Before You Listen

Work with your partner. Draw lines to match the definitions on the left with the words on the right. The first one is done for you.

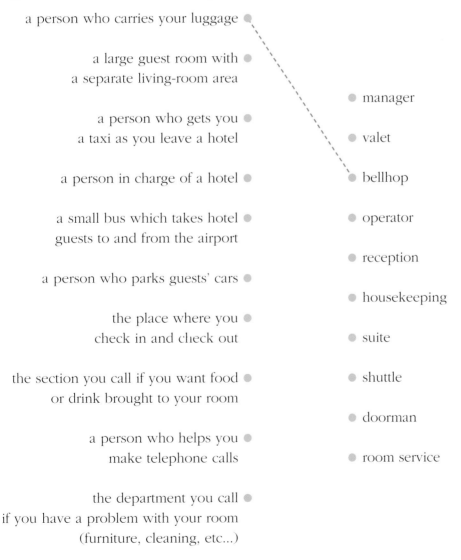

a person who carries your luggage

a large guest room with a separate living-room area

manager

a person who gets you a taxi as you leave a hotel

valet

a person in charge of a hotel

bellhop

a small bus which takes hotel guests to and from the airport

operator

reception

a person who parks guests' cars

housekeeping

the place where you check in and check out

suite

the section you call if you want food or drink brought to your room

shuttle

doorman

a person who helps you make telephone calls

room service

the department you call if you have a problem with your room (furniture, cleaning, etc…)

Listen to four conversations. Look at the pictures. Write the number of the conversation under each picture.

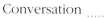

Conversation .....

Conversation .....

Conversation .....

Conversation .....

Check your answers with a partner.

Listen to Conversation 4 again. Place a check (✓) next to the requests Mr. Campbell made when he reserved the room.

☐ a non-smoking room
☐ a suite
☐ a king-sized double bed
☐ a corner room
☐ a room with a view of the ocean

Check your answers with your partner.

▸Listening Clinic One: Weak Vowels

Sometimes speakers say vowels weakly.

> **Example** : I'd like to make a complaint. → I'd like tø make ∅ complaint.

Listen and complete the dialogue.

A: What seems .... the problem, sir?

B: .... balcony window. .... can't open it.

A: Sorry, ma'am. .... send someone right away.

B: Thanks very much.

Check your answers with your partner. Now say the dialogue together.

▸Practice!

Work with your partner. Follow the prompts and have two conversations. Take turns to be the guest and the check-in clerk.

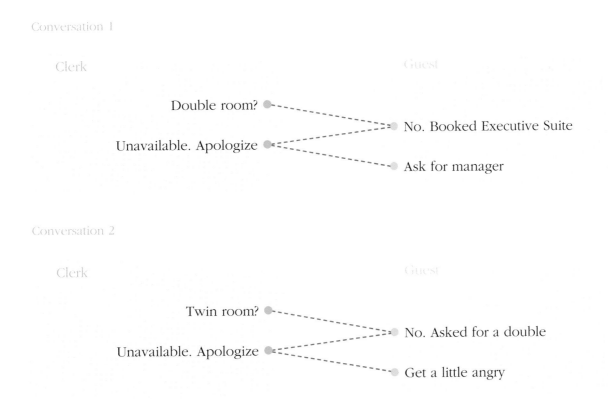

Conversation 1

Clerk   Guest

Double room? ●------
                                                    ●== No. Booked Executive Suite
Unavailable. Apologize ●==

                                                    ● Ask for manager

Conversation 2

Clerk   Guest

Twin room? ●------
                                                    ●== No. Asked for a double
Unavailable. Apologize ●==

                                                    ● Get a little angry

▶Now Listen Back

CD Tracks: 31, 32, 33, 34

Listen to the conversations again and answer the question. Circle *Yes* or *No*.

Does the guest accept the apology?

Conversation 1	Yes	No
Conversation 2	Yes	No
Conversation 3	Yes	No
Conversation 4	Yes	No

Check your answers with your partner.

▶Listening Clinic Two: Weak Vowels

CD Track: 36

Listen to six sentences. How many words are there? Circle your answer. Contractions (for example *she's* or *I'm*) count as two words.

1.	5	6	7
2.	5	6	7
3.	5	6	7
4.	6	7	8
5.	6	7	8
6.	6	7	8

Now turn to page 88. Check your answers and say the sentences.

▶Try It Out!

Work with your partner. Look at the list of complaints that a guest in a hotel might make. Imagine you are the guest. What do you want the manager to do? Imagine you are the manager. What will you do? Discuss your ideas.

- the shower doesn't work
- the mini-bar is empty
- the receptionist was rude
- bed isn't made
- the valet scratched your car
- the people next door are noisy

Roleplay
Work with a new partner. Take turns to be the guest and the manager. Roleplay some of the problems. Can you find a solution?

▶In Your Own Time

Turn to pages 104 and 105 and complete the word list. Use your dictionary if you want to. Use the CD at the back of your book and listen to the recordings in this unit again. The script for this unit is on pages 86, 87 and 88.

Did you see the paper?

⊹Let's Start!

Work with your partner. Use your background knowledge. Draw lines to match the numbers on the right to the topics on the left.

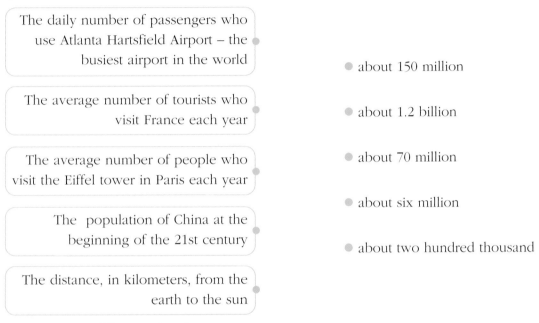

The daily number of passengers who use Atlanta Hartsfield Airport – the busiest airport in the world

The average number of tourists who visit France each year

The average number of people who visit the Eiffel tower in Paris each year

The population of China at the beginning of the 21st century

The distance, in kilometers, from the earth to the sun

● about 150 million

● about 1.2 billion

● about 70 million

● about six million

● about two hundred thousand

Check your answers with your teacher.

⊹Before You Listen

Work with your partner. Draw lines to match the numbers written in words on the left with the numbers written in figures on the right. The first one is done for you.

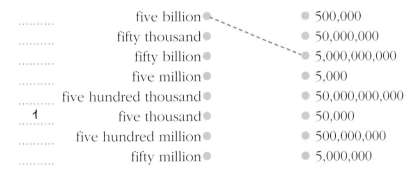

....	five billion ●	● 500,000
....	fifty thousand ●	● 50,000,000
....	fifty billion ●	● 5,000,000,000
....	five million ●	● 5,000
....	five hundred thousand ●	● 50,000,000,000
1	five thousand ●	● 50,000
....	five hundred million ●	● 500,000,000
....	fifty million ●	● 5,000,000

Now cover the right-hand column. Put the numbers written as words in order from *1* (the smallest number) to *8* (the biggest number). The first one is done for you.

Work with your partner. Cover the left-hand column. Take turns to point to some of the figures. Try and say the number that your partner points to.

▶Let's Listen!

Listen to four conversations. Write the number of the conversation next to its title. There is one title too many.

Title

.... HOW CAN THEY ALL FIT?

.... TIME IS MONEY. MONEY IS TIME

.... ARE WE MAKING ANY MONEY?

.... A GREAT NEW JOB

.... IT'S GOING TO BE A SMALLER WORLD

▶Listen Again

CD Track: 40

Listen to Conversation 4 again. Draw lines to match the information on the left with the dollar amount on the right.

The amount of money Manchester ●
United will pay Roma to buy Basil Panini

● 130,000

● 8,000,000

Basil Panini's weekly salary at ●
Manchester United

● 130,000,000

The total amount of money ●
Basil Panini will earn during five
years at Manchester United

● 70,000,000

● 80,000,000

▶Listening Clinic One: Lost Sounds

CD Track: 41

Sounds in and at the end of words are sometimes not spoken. They are lost.

| Example | Half pas**t** seven → Half pas~~t~~ seven |

Listen to the dialogue. Circle the places where sounds are *lost*.

A: I got a great deal on this car.

B: How much did it cost?

A: They usually cost 30,000 dollars, but I got mine for twenty-three.

B: So you saved seven thousand dollars. Wow!

Check your answers with your partner. Now say the dialogue together.

►Practice!

Work with your partner. Follow the prompts and talk about the two news stories. Use the information in the boxes. Take turns to tell the stories.

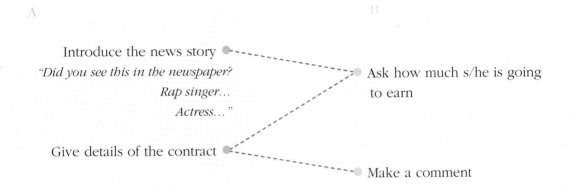

A

Introduce the news story
"Did you see this in the newspaper?
Rap singer...
Actress..."

Give details of the contract

B

Ask how much s/he is going
to earn

Make a comment

News Story for Student A

Rap singer Tuff Booty has just signed a new record contract with EMV Records.

Contract Details
- one album per year for five years
- $15,000,000 per album plus royalties
- Total earnings: $100,000,000

News Story for Student B

Actress Lily Lee has agreed to stay for one more year with the hit TV series *Home*.

Contract Details
- 30 shows per year
- $850,000 per show plus bonuses
- Total earnings: $30,000,000

►Now Listen Back

CD Track: 37, 38, 39, 40

Listen to the conversations again. Circle the topic which the numbers refer to.

Conversation 1	People	Money	Distance	Cameras
Conversation 2	People	Money	Distance	Cameras
Conversation 3	People	Money	Distance	Cameras
Conversation 4	People	Money	Distance	Cameras

Check your answers with your partner.

Work with your partner. Look at the sentences. Circle places where sounds may be *lost*.

1. He earned ten thousand pounds for ten minutes work.
2. This idea could be worth millions of dollars.
3. They will invest more than eighty million in the next few months.
4. Venus is forty million kilometers from Earth. It's our closest neighbor.
5. The world's population may reach nine billion in the twenty-first century.
6. Recently, the stock market has been doing badly.

Listen and check. Now say the sentences.

Try It Out!

Work with your partner. Student A: Turn to page 84. Student B: Turn to page 90.

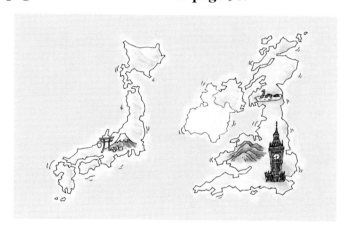

In Your Own Time

Turn to pages 105 and 106 and complete the word list. Use your dictionary if you want to. Use the CD at the back of your book and listen to the recordings in this unit again. The script for this unit is on pages 88 and 89.

We can't have any mistakes

⊹Let's Start!

Work with your partner. Look at the picture. The bank is going to be robbed in a few minutes. In the picture, there are the seven members of the gang. Who do you think they are?

⊹Before You Listen

Work with your partner. Draw lines and match the statements on the left with their meaning on the right. One is done for you.

Statement		Meaning
The gang leader *might* be the man with the briefcase	●	● Definitely yes
The guys on the motorbike *are probably* lookout men	●	● Good chance
The bank *is going to* be robbed	●	● Definitely no
The robbers *will probably* have guns	●	● Small chance
The security guard *might* stop the robbers	●	
The police *won't* come in time to stop the robbery	●	

Look at the picture again. Talk about what you think is happening. Talk about what you think might/will probably/is going to happen.

Let's Listen!

CD Track: 43

Listen to the conversation. The bank robbers are talking about their plan. Look at the picture and do the following:

- Circle the members of the gang.
- Place a cross (X) next to the gang leader.
- Circle the bank manager.
- Draw the security guard's route to the bank.

Check your answers with your partner.

Listen Again

CD Track: 43

Listen to the conversation again. Circle the phrase to show how likely the following events are.

Event	How Likely?	
start making noise before 9:15	No Chance	Small Chance
manager arriving first	Good Chance	Definitely
manager arriving at 8:10	Small Chance	Good Chance
tellers arriving after 8:45	No Chance	Good Chance
tellers using the side entrance	No Chance	Small Chance
Jenkins in the bank by 9:10	Good Chance	Definitely
bank opening at 9:30	Good Chance	Definitely
starting the getaway cars at 9:40	No Chance	Good Chance
robbers carrying guns	No Chance	Small Chance

Listening Clinic One: Lost Sounds

CD Track: 44

Sometimes speakers don't pronounce all the sounds in the words. Sounds can be lost.

> **Example** I didn't see him last night. → I didn see im las nigh.
> The /t/ sounds and the /h/ are lost

Listen to the dialogue. Draw a line through any /t/ sounds which are *lost*.

A: Hey, Bobbie. What time do we start?
B: What? You forgot? Rocky, we've been over it and over it.
A: Yeah, I know. I just forgot.
B: Okay. We start at eight.
A: What was that?
B: Eight, Rocky! Eight.

Check your answers with your partner. Now say the dialogue together.

⊡Practice!

Work with your partner. Look at the pictures. What might/will probably/ is going to/won't happen?

Compare your ideas with another pair.

⊡Now Listen Back

CD Track: 43

Listen to the conversation again. Put the events in the correct order. The first one is done for you.

- ..... the bank robbery starts
- ..... the security guard arrives at work
- _1_ the bank manager arrives at work
- ..... Billy and Benny G start their engines
- ..... the tellers arrive at work
- ..... Bob leaves the coffee shop
- ..... Algernon's team starts making noise

Work with your partner. Look at the sentences. Draw a line through any /t/ or /h/ sounds that may be *lost*.

1. I might get lost if I don't have a map.
2. I can't see him tomorrow night.
3. We'll probably stop in at the Service Counter.
4. He's not going to eat some more, is he?
5. The plan's pretty good, isn't it?
6. I don't think I can meet her tonight.

Listen and check. Now say the sentences.

⊕Try It Out!

Work in a group of three. You are detectives. You have found some of Johnny's notes about the gang's plans for after the robbery.

- What do you think they might do?
- What do you think they'll probably do?
- What do you think they're going to do?
- What do you think they won't do?

Discuss your ideas in your group then compare them with a student from another group.

> The Getaway Plan?
>
> Algernon's team: subway downtown. Problems? bikes–cycle downtown.
> Me, Billy: Car #1
> Bob, Benny G: Car #2
> Money: Car #1
> Car #1: highway to interstate?
> side roads to cabin?
> Car #2: drive to harbor.
> Boat to cabin.
> Reach cabin 2:00pm? By 4:00pm
> Split up the money?
> Bury the money?
> Benny G & Billy: Venice beach, 10 days
> Bob & me: Atlantic City 3 days? 4 days?
> Algernon: home to mom
> Meet up again in Mexico ir

⊕In Your Own Time

Turn to page 106 and complete the word list. Use your dictionary if you want to.
Use the CD at the back of your book and listen to the recordings in this unit again. The script for this unit is on pages 90 and 91.

How are we feeling today?

Let's Start!

Work with your partner. Check (✓) the best answer to complete the sentences.

■ A *headache*, a *sore throat*, and a *high temperature*, are all .... of a cold.
   ☐ cures   ☐ symptoms   ☐ treatments

■ A *rash* is a medical problem which affects your ....
   ☐ eyes   ☐ teeth   ☐ skin

■ A person suffering from *insomnia* has difficulty ....
   ☐ talking   ☐ walking   ☐ sleeping

■ If you get *indigestion*, you have probably ....
   ☐ eaten too much   ☐ talked too much   ☐ slept too much

■ If a part of your body is *swollen*, it is ....
   ☐ bigger than usual ☐ smaller than usual ☐ a different color than usual

Check your answers with your teacher.

Before You Listen

Work with your partner. Put a word from the box into each space. (Some words can go in more than one space).

■ headache	■ chest	■ bone	■ wrist	■ skin
■ cut	■ temperature	■ throat	■ cold	■ nose

a sore ....   a pain in my ....
a high ....   a runny ....
a sprained ....   itchy ....
a broken ....   a heavy ....
a splitting ....   a deep ....

Compare your answers with your partner.

Listen to four conversations. Write the number of the conversation next to the correct patient.

Which conversation does not have a picture?   1   2   3   4

Listen to the conversations again. Place a check (✓) against the symptoms you hear.

- ☐ a headache
- ☐ a swollen wrist
- ☐ high blood pressure
- ☐ a rash
- ☐ chest pain
- ☐ toothache
- ☐ a runny nose

Check your answers with your partner.

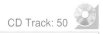

Listening Clinic One: Requests And Commands   CD Track: 50

When the speaker wants to make a request, the intonation often goes up.

When the speaker wants to give a command, the intonation often goes down.

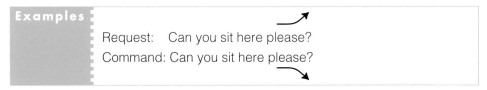

Examples

Request: Can you sit here please?

Command: Can you sit here please?

Listen to the dialogue. Circle the arrow to show if the speaker's voice goes up and is *making a request* or goes down and is *giving a command.*

A: Could you try to move it for me?   ↗   ↘

B: It's a bit painful, doctor.

A: Try to move your toes one at a time.   ↗   ↘

B: Ouch!

A: Okay. Could you try with the other foot now?   ↗   ↘

Check your answers with your partner. Now say the dialogue together.

Practice!

Work with your partner. Use the ideas below and practice giving advice. Use the following dialogue to help you. Take turns to be A and B.

A: What's the matter?

B: I've got a really bad   .

A: That's too bad. ⎡ Why don't you   ?

⎣ Maybe you should   .

B: Hmm. Good idea. Maybe I will.

Problem	Advice
cold	hot honey and lemon drink
backache	*shiatsu* massage
hangover	strong black coffee
muscle pain	really hot bath

Listen to the conversations again. Circle *Yes* if the doctor gives the patient advice. Circle *No* if she does not.

Conversation 1	Yes	No
Conversation 2	Yes	No
Conversation 3	Yes	No
Conversation 4	Yes	No

Check your answers with your partner.

∙Listening Clinic Two: Requests And Commands CD Track: 51

Listen to the sentences. Circle the arrows to show if the intonation goes up or down.

1. Can you come with me please?   ↗   ↘
2. Can I see your boarding pass?   ↗   ↘
3. Would you mind smoking over there?   ↗   ↘
4. Can I have some water please?   ↗   ↘
5. Can you write that down for me?   ↗   ↘
6. Could you look after my bag for a minute? ↗   ↘

Listen and check. Now say the sentences.

∙Try It Out!

Work in two groups, Group A and Group B.

Group A

You are doctors. Student B is a patient who is having trouble sleeping. Prepare some suggestions for your patient. Do the following:

- Greet the patient and make him/her relaxed.
- Ask what the problem is.
- Find out how long the patient has had the problem.
- Try to find out the cause of the problem, (stress at school/work? money worries? family difficulties? etc...).
- Give the patient some advice.
- Ask the patient to come back and see you.

Fill in the sheet with information about the patient.

```
Patient's Name: ....................................................
Problem: ..............................................................
Started: ...............................................................
Reasons for Problem: ..........................................
            ...............................................................
Advice: ................................................................
Next Appointment: ..............................................
```

You are patients. Recently you have been unable to sleep at night. Prepare to answer the doctor's questions. Complete the sheet with information about your problem.

```
Problem: _Can't sleep well_ ..................................
How long: ...........................................................
Possible Reasons: ...............................................
            ...............................................................
            ...............................................................
```

Now work with a partner from the other group. Roleplay the doctor/patient conversation.

In Your Own Time

Turn to pages 106 and 107 and complete the word list. Use your dictionary if you want to. Use the CD at the back of your book and listen to the recordings in this unit again. The script for this unit is on pages 91, 92 and 93.

Could you give me a hand?

▶Let's Start!

Work with your partner. Look at the situations. Place a check (✓) in the box to show the best way to make the request in each situation.

- At the counter in a coffee shop to a close friend:
  - ☐ Do you think you could pass the sugar, please?
  - ☐ Pass the sugar, will you?
  - ☐ Would you mind passing the sugar?

- At the counter in a coffee shop alone. Ask a stranger sitting beside you:
  - ☐ Pass the sugar, will you?
  - ☐ Could you pass the sugar, please?
  - ☐ I wonder if you could possibly pass me the sugar.

- At an airline check-in counter:
  - ☐ I'd like a window seat please, if you have one.
  - ☐ Give me a seat by the window.
  - ☐ Do you think there's any chance of me being able to get a seat by a window?

- A parent talking to their ten-year-old child:
  - ☐ Could you stop biting your fingernails, please?
  - ☐ Would you mind not biting your fingernails?
  - ☐ Stop biting your fingernails.

- A ten-year-old child talking to their mother:
  - ☐ Can I have some ice cream?
  - ☐ Would you mind giving me some ice cream?
  - ☐ Give me some ice cream.

Compare your answers with another pair.

⊹Before You Listen

Work with your partner and do the three exercises below.

Expressions

Look at these expressions. Write *R* if the person is *requesting* something. Write *P* if the person is asking for *permission* to do something. Two are done for you.

.... Could you close the door, please?

.... Would you mind if I closed the window?

.... Can I close the window?

  R   Do you think you could possibly close the door, please?

.... Close the door, will you?

.... Would you mind closing the door, please?

  P   Is it okay if I close the window?

.... Do you mind if I close the window?

Which are formal? Which are less formal?

Replies to Requests

Look at these replies. Do they *agree* to the request, or *refuse* the request?
Write *A* (agree) or *R* (refuse) next to each reply. One is done for you.

.... Okay.

.... Sure.

.... No problem.

  R   Why me? You're nearer.

.... Of course.

.... Well, I'd rather not.

Replies to Permission

Look at these replies. Do they *give* permission or *refuse* permission?
Write *G* (give) or *R* (refuse) next to each reply. One is done for you.

.... Go ahead.

.... I'd rather you didn't.

  G   Please do.

.... Actually, I'm trying to get some fresh air.

.... Good idea.

Check your answers with another pair.

▶ Let's Listen!

Listen to four conversations. Draw lines to match the conversation to what each child wants to do.

- play a video game
Conversation 1 ●
- watch TV
Conversation 2 ●
- borrow some money
Conversation 3 ●
- use the family car
Conversation 4 ●
- have some ice cream
- go out to meet friends

Check your answers with your partner.

▶ Listen Again

CD Track: 55

Listen to Conversation 4 again. Place a check (✓) next to the things Claire is asked to do.

☐ turn off the TV ☐ clean her room ☐ stop using the telephone
☐ wash some clothes ☐ do her homework ☐ help with the cooking

Check your answers with your partner.

▶ Listening Clinic One: Stressing Important Information

CD Track: 56

Sometimes speakers put heavy stress on words to show they are very important.

 Actually, I wasn't <u>born</u> in Vancouver, but I went to <u>school</u> there.

Listen to the dialogue. Underline the words which have *heavy stress*.

A: Billy! I said turn that TV off, not turn it down. It's time for bed.

B: But, Mom, you let me stay up late last night. Why can't I stay up late tonight?

A: Last night was Saturday night. Tonight is Sunday night, and you've got school tomorrow.

B: But I want to…

A: No arguing. It's time for bed.

Check your answers with your partner. Now say the dialogue together.

⊹Practice!

Work with your partner. Follow the prompts and roleplay two conversations between a parent and a child.

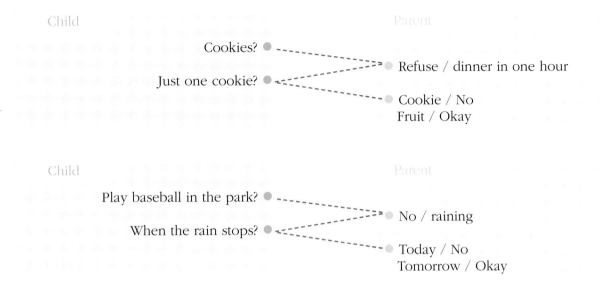

⊹Now Listen Back

CD Tracks: 52, 53, 54, 55

Listen to the four conversations again. Circle *Yes* if the parent agrees to the child's request. Circle *No* if s/he does not.

Conversation 1   Yes   No
Conversation 2   Yes   No
Conversation 3   Yes   No
Conversation 4   Yes   No

Check your answers with your partner.

⊹Listening Clinic Two: Stressing Important Information   CD Track: 57

Work with your partner. Look at the sentences. Underline words you think may have *heavy stress*. The first one is done for you.

1. You can't go <u>today</u>, but you can go <u>tomorrow</u>.
2. You let her do it, but you never let me do it.
3. You're supposed to be reading school books, not comic books.
4. Ten dollars would be okay, but I really need twenty.
5. He's more than just a good dad, he's a good friend, too.
6. It's ten o'clock. You said you'd be home at nine.

Listen and check. Now say the sentences.

▶Try It Out!

Work in two groups, A and B. Look at your situation. Decide with the people in your group what you are going to say.

Group A

You are students and you are starting a part-time job at a coffee shop. Find out from your new boss if you can:

- start late on some days
- keep any tips you get
- eat food for free
- finish early on some days
- use the phone for private calls
- sit with friends when they come

Group B

You are owners of a coffee shop. Explain to your new waiter/waitress these extra things you want them to do in their job:

- clean the tables
- wash the dishes
- work late sometimes
- clean the toilets
- start early sometimes
- hand out advertising flyers

Now work with a partner from the other group and roleplay the conversation.

▶In Your Own Time

Turn to page 107 and complete the word list. Use your dictionary if you want to.
Use the CD at the back of your book and listen to the recordings in this unit again. The script for this unit is on pages 93 and 94.

Unit 11   This is the six o'clock news

Let's Start!

Work with your partner. Ask and answer the questions.

Did you watch the TV news this morning?

What is the biggest news story this week?

What's your favorite news channel? Why?

When do you usually watch the news?

What kinds of stories are usually on the news?

Words

Work with your partner. Put three words or phrases into each of the news categories.

Sport	The Economy	Crime	Natural Disasters
....	....	....	....
....	....	....	....
....	....	....	....

- arrest
- champion
- interest rates
- tournament
- stock market
- title
- inflation
- escape
- earthquake
- typhoon
- flood
- kidnap

Before You Listen

Work with your partner. Look at the news stories. Imagine you are the director of a radio station. In which order should the stories appear on tonight's news?

..... a kidnapped girl in Hong Kong is rescued

..... the New York Stock Market falls sharply

..... a powerful typhoon hits Japan

..... a girl becomes the youngest person to win a tennis tournament

Compare your ideas with another pair.

Listen to the news report. Number the stories in the order they appear.

..... kidnapped girl

..... New York stock prices

..... typhoon

..... youngest winner

Check your answers with your partner.

Is the news report order the same as yours?

▶Listen Again

CD Track: 58

Listen to the News Story 1 again. Draw lines to match the number on the left to its topic on the right.

160 ●   ● damaged homes

several hundred ●   ● helpers from Tokyo

700 ●   ● amount of rainfall

500 ●   ● speed of wind

200 ●   ● people made homeless

Check your answers with your partner.

▶Listening Clinic One: Helping Sounds

CD Track: 59

When a word ends in a vowel and the next word starts with a vowel, a helping sound comes between them so they are easier to say.

Examples	Alaska and China → Alaska-*r*-and China
	She isn't here. → She-*y*-isn't here.
	I want to open my presents. → I want to-*w*-open my presents.

Listen to the dialogue. A *helping sound* will appear between the vowels in bold. Decide if the sound is *w*, *y*, or *r*.

A: Did you se**e a**nything interesting in the paper?

B: Not much. I don't like this paper much.

A: **I a**gree. It's to**o e**xpensive as well.

B: The sports section's okay.

A: Not really. It only covers Americ**a a**nd Canada.

Check your answers with your partner. Now say the dialogue together.

⊁Practice!

Work with your partner. Look at the pictures. Put them in the correct order to make a story.

Part 1

Part 2

Part 3

Tell the story together.

⊁Now Listen Back

CD Track: 58

Listen to the four news stories again. Circle *Good* if the story is about good news. Circle *Bad* if the story is about bad news.

News Story 1	Good	Bad
News Story 2	Good	Bad
News Story 3	Good	Bad
News Story 4	Good	Bad

Compare your answers with your partner.

Work with your partner. Look at the sentences. Circle places where you think *helping sounds* may appear. Decide if the helping sound is *w*, *r*, or *y*.

1. Can I ask you another question?
2. The country's had two elections this year already.
3. I can't remember the exact place.
4. The reporter had a camera inside his bag.
5. I'd like to go over the details once more.
6. I think I left my umbrella on the train.

Listen and check. Now say the sentences.

⊩Try It Out!

Work in a group of three. Choose *one* of the news stories. Make notes and prepare a news report. Your story should answer these questions:

- ■ What happened?
- ■ Who did it happen to?
- ■ When did it happen?
- ■ How or why did it happen?
- ■ Where did it happen?

Postman Bites Dog!

Dragon Captured on Remote Island

Bank Robbers Escape with $15 Million

30 Injured in Highway Bus Crash

**Now work with a new student. Tell your news stories to each other.
Ask questions.**

⊩In Your Own Time

**Turn to pages 107 and 108 and complete the word list. Use your dictionary if you want to.
Use the CD at the back of your book and listen to the recordings in this unit again. The script for this unit is on pages 94 and 95.**

Unit 12   Can I take a message?

▸Let's Start!

Work on your own. Look at the sentences. Try to guess the correct information about your partner. Check (✓) the word or phrase to complete each sentence.

■ My partner .... a cell phone.
- ☐ owns
- ☐ doesn't own

■ My partner spends .... a week on the phone.
- ☐ less time than me
- ☐ about the same time as me
- ☐ more time than me

■ My partner made .... phone calls yesterday.
- ☐ less than 5
- ☐ between 5 and 10
- ☐ more than 10

■ My partner .... made a phone call in English during the last month.
- ☐ has
- ☐ hasn't

■ My partner .... how to say *Could you ask him to call me back?* in his/her own language.
- ☐ knows
- ☐ doesn't know

Now ask your partner questions to check your guesses.

■ Do you…?
■ How many…?

How many of your guesses were correct?

Work with your partner. Look at the list of questions in the left column. Write *C* (caller) next to the phrases spoken by the person making the call, or *M* (message taker) next to the person who receives the call and takes a message.

.... Would you like to leave a message?

.... Have you any idea what time she'll be back?

.... Could you give him a message for me?

.... Does he know your number?

.... Could you spell that for me, please?

.... Could you tell him it's urgent?

.... Will he be back later?

.... Can I ask who's calling?

- Yes, It's G-I-L-E-S.
- I think around 4:30.
- Yes, this is David Watts from Weller Cosmetics.
- No, I'm afraid he's out for the rest of the day.
- Certainly.
- No thanks. I'll call back later.
- Yes, of course. I'll get him to call you as soon as he's free.
- I think so, but I'll give it to you anyway. It's .....

Now draw lines and match each question with its answer from the right-hand column. Work with a partner. Check your answers by practicing each question and answer.

▸Let's Listen!   CD Tracks: 61, 62, 63, 64

Listen to four telephone conversations. Write the number of the conversation next to the main point of the call.

..... Please tell her I'll be an hour late.

..... I'll call again at 2 o'clock.

..... I'll call her on her cell phone.

..... Could you ask him to call me?

..... I'll call again tomorrow.

..... Could you ask him to email me?

Check your answers with your partner.

▸Listen Again   CD Track: 64

Listen to Conversation 4 again. Place a check (✓) next to the information that Jason should give to Mr Fairweather.

☐ Mr. Fern wants Mr. Fairweather to email him.

☐ Mr. Fern wants to arrange a meeting next week.

☐ Mr. Fern wants to have the meeting on Wednesday.

☐ Mr. Fern works for Northern Bank.

☐ Mr. Fern will call again later.

Check your answers with your partner.

⊪Listening Clinic One: Weak Vowels

Sometimes speakers say vowels weakly.

> **Example** : I want to go to Panama. → uh wana go du Panuma.

Listen to the dialogue. Circle words where vowels are spoken *weakly*.

A: Can I speak to Bob Taylor, please?

B: Can I ask who's calling?

A: Yes. This is Carol James.

B: Just a moment, Ms. James... Um... I'm afraid he's out of the office today.

A: I see. Can you get him to call me back tomorrow?

B: Certainly.

Check your answers with your partner. Now say the dialogue together.

⊪Practice!

Work with your partner. Number the sentences and put the conversation in the correct order. The first one is done for you.

.... Yes, please. Could you ask him to call Brian Hart. That's H-A-R-T.

.... Thanks a lot. Goodbye.

.... I'm afraid Mr. Taylor is out of the office at the moment. Can I take a message?

.... It's 706-5451.

__1__ Good morning. Temple Investments. How can I help you?

.... Goodbye.

.... Okay, Mr. Hart. I'll get Mr. Taylor to call you as soon as he gets back.

.... Certainly, Mr. Hart. And what's your number?

.... Good morning. May I speak to Martin Taylor, please?

Now practice the dialogue together two or three times.
Close your books. Can you remember the dialogue?

⊹Now Listen Back

Listen to the conversations again. Circle *Yes* or *No* to answer the question.

Do the caller and the person answering the phone know each other?

| Conversation 1 | Yes | No | Conversation 3 | Yes | No |
| Conversation 2 | Yes | No | Conversation 4 | Yes | No |

Check your answers with your partner.

⊹Listening Clinic Two: Weak Vowels

Work with your partner. Look at the sentences. Circle any words where vowels may be spoken *weakly*.

1. I'll get him to call you as soon as he's free.
2. I'm sorry, she's out on a job at the moment.
3. This is Tom Shepard.
4. I'd like to speak to Mr. Fairweather, please.
5. I want to arrange a meeting with Mr. Fairweather.
6. She's out, I'm afraid. Can I take a message?

Listen and check. Now say the sentences.

⊹Try It Out!

Work with your partner. You are going to do two telephone roleplays. Do not look at your partner's information.

Roleplay One

Student A:

You are the caller. You want to speak to John Dawson of Samson International. Use the information below and leave a message.

Your name:	Use your real name.
Your company:	Cyber Solutions
Your phone number:	831-7294
Your message:	Need to cancel tomorrow's meeting. Please phone me to arrange a new time.

Speech bubbles: "Mayfair Properties. How can I help you?" / "I'd like to speak to Mike Daley, please."

Student B:

You are answering the call (you speak first).
You work for Samson International. You are
John Dawson's assistant. Mr. Dawson is out of
the office. Take a message. Write the
information on the form on the right.

While You Were Out ...

Caller's name:...
Company: ....
Number: ....
Message: ....
....
....
....
....
....

Roleplay Two

Student A:

You are answering the call (you speak first).
You work for Mayfair Properties. You are Mike
Daly's assistant. Mr. Daly is in a meeting. Take
a message. Write the information on the form
on the right.

While You Were Out ...

Caller's name:...
Company: ....
Number: ....
Message: ....
....
....

Student B:

You are the caller. You want to speak to Mike Daly of Mayfair Properties. Use the information below
and leave a message.

Your name:	Use your real name.
Your company:	Boston Management
Your phone number:	510-779-3691
Your message:	Want to arrange a meeting.
	Please phone tomorrow, before 3 p.m. if possible.

⊡ In Your Own Time

Turn to page 108 and complete the word list. Use your dictionary if you want to.
Use the CD at the back of your book and listen to the recordings in this unit again. The script
for this unit is on pages 95 and 96.

How do you work this?

▸Let's Start!

Work in a group of three. Look at the pictures. Ask and answer the questions.

- What are these pictures of?
- Which of these items do you own?
- How often do you use each item?
- Do you find any of them difficult to use?

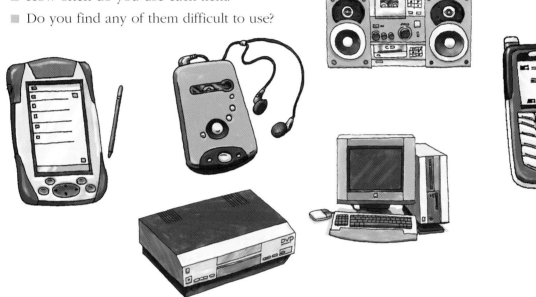

▸Before You Listen

Work with your partner. Draw lines to match the verbs on the left with the words and phrases on the write. The first one is done for you.

Verbs	Words and Phrases
Press	the volume level
Dub	the money in the slot
Switch on	the knob
Scroll down	the button
Enter	the icon
Adjust	the CD
Click	the list
Turn	the number on the keypad
Put	the power

Let's Listen!

CD Tracks: 67, 68, 69, 70

Listen to the conversations. Write the number of the conversation next to the correct picture. There is one picture too many.

Check your answers with your partner.

Listen Again

CD Track: 70

Listen to Conversation 4 again. Number the steps in the correct order. The first one is done for you.

.... Press the *Send* button

.... Enter the *G-code* number

.... Press the *G-code* button

.... Press the *Program* button

__1__ Put a blank tape in the machine

.... Press the *Timer Set* button

Check your answers with your partner.

Speakers sometimes put heavy stress on words to show they are more important.

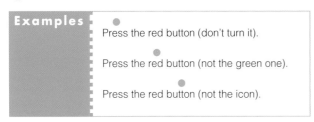

Examples
- Press the red button (don't turn it).
- Press the red button (not the green one).
- Press the red button (not the icon).

Listen to the dialogue. Underline the words the speakers use heavy stress to show they are *more important*.

A: Click on the right button, then a dialogue box will come up.
B: Like this?
A: No, no. The right button.
B: Oh, like this?
A: Yeah. Now select *Save to Disk*.
B: This?
A: No. *Save to Disk*.

Check your answers with your partner.
Now say the dialogue together.

⯈Practice!

Work with your partner. Look at the steps explaining how to use a photocopier. Number them in order from *1* (do first) to *8* (do last). The first one is done for you.

.... Select the paper size
.... Make sure it's the right way up
.... Put the cover down
.... Place the paper on the glass
.... Press *All Clear*
.... Enter the number of copies you want
...1... Lift the cover
.... Press the *Start* button

Now explain how to use a photocopier to each other. Take turns giving and following instructions. Use the prompts below to help you.

Giving Instructions

First you …
Then you should…
Next you need to…
Now…

Following Instructions

Yeah
I see
Okay
Like this?

Now close your books. Give each other the instructions once more. How much can you remember?

Now Listen Back

CD Tracks: 67, 68, 69, 70

Listen to the conversations again. Circle *Yes* if the person can follow the instructions. Circle *No* if s/he cannot understand the instructions.

Conversation 1	Yes	No
Conversation 2	Yes	No
Conversation 3	Yes	No
Conversation 4	Yes	No

Listening Clinic Two: Stressing Important Information CD Track: 72

Work with your partner. Look at the sentences. Underline the words where the speaker may use heavy stress to show they are *more important*.

1. Well, that's a whole lot better than my old machine.
2. Do you want to dub the whole album?
3. Do you see the arrow on the side?
4. Now press the button with the red dot on it.
5. How can I remember all that?
6. Now take the remote control and press the program button.

Listen and check. Now say the sentences.

Work with your partner and play this guessing game.

Student A

Look at the pictures. How do you use these machines? Explain to your partner. Do not tell your partner which machine you are talking about.

Student B

Listen to your partner. Can you guess which machine your partner is talking about?

Take turns to be A and B.

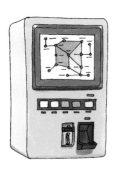

▣ buying a railway ticket

▣ withdrawing some money

▣ sending a fax

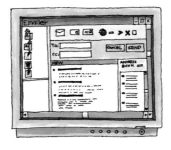

▣ buying a coffee with extra sugar

▣ replying to an email

▣ making coffee

▶In Your Own Time

Turn to pages 108 and 109 and complete the word list. Use your dictionary if you want to. Use the CD at the back of your book and listen to the recordings in this unit again. The script for this unit is on pages 97 and 98.

Things have changed

▶Let's Start!

Work with your partner. Look at the pictures. The top picture shows the town 30 years ago. The bottom picture shows it today. What has changed? How many differences can you find?

30 years ago

Today

Check your answers with another pair.

▶Before You Listen

Work with your partner. Draw lines to match the phrases in Column A with the phrases in Column B to make a complete sentence. The first one is done for you.

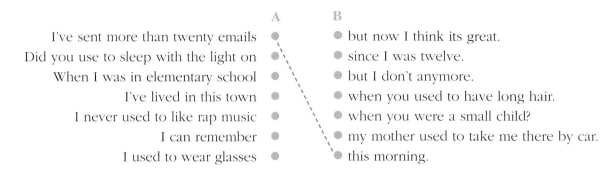

	A	B
I've sent more than twenty emails	●	● but now I think its great.
Did you use to sleep with the light on	●	● since I was twelve.
When I was in elementary school	●	● but I don't anymore.
I've lived in this town	●	● when you used to have long hair.
I never used to like rap music	●	● when you were a small child?
I can remember	●	● my mother used to take me there by car.
I used to wear glasses	●	● this morning.

Can you think of some things you used to do but don't do now?

▶Let's Listen!   CD Tracks: 73, 74, 75

Listen to three conversations. Place a check (✓) to choose the best title for each conversation.

Conversation 1 ☐ I'm going to stop smoking   ☐ I'm glad I stopped smoking

Conversation 2 ☐ The old town's really changed ☐ It's good to be home

Conversation 3 ☐ I never really loved you   ☐ We're not the same people anymore

Check your answers with your partner.

▶Listen Again   CD Track: 75

Listen to Conversation 3 again. Draw lines to show how the man and woman think the other has changed.

● used to be more romantic

The man thinks that the woman ●   ● never used to complain all the time

The woman thinks that the man ●   ● never used to be boring

● has put on a lot of weight

Check your answers with your partner.

⏵Listening Clinic One: Mixed Sounds

CD Track: 76

Sometimes when two consonant sounds come together, one at the end of one word and one at the beginning of the next, they mix and make a new sound.

Example	Where did you use to live? → Whereju use to live?

Listen to the dialogue. Circle places where sounds *mix*.

A: So what do you think about the old town?

B: Well, it's great being back.

A: It's changed a lot you know.

B: What do you mean?

A: Do you remember the Odeon theater, on First Avenue?

B: Yeah. I saw it yesterday. Now it's an office building.

Check your answers with your partner. Now say the dialogue together.

⏵Practice!

Work with your partner. Look at the pictures. They show the same man, fifteen years ago and today.

15 Years ago

Today

Student A: Turn to page 86. Student B: Turn to page 92.

⏵Now Listen Back

CD Tracks: 73, 74, 75

Listen to the conversations again. Circle the word to answer the question.

Are things better or worse than they used to be?

Conversation 1	Better	Worse
Conversation 2	Better	Worse
Conversation 3	Better	Worse

Compare your answers with your partner.

Listening Clinic Two: Mixed Sounds

 CD Track: 77

Work with your partner. Look at the sentences. Circle the places where sounds may *mix*.

1. What are you going to do?
2. Who did you say we were meeting?
3. You used to play the piano, didn't you?
4. How about you?
5. What did you use to play?
6. Didn't you say she was coming at seven?

Listen and check. Now say the sentences.

Try It Out!

Work on your own. Look at the table. Write some information about yourself in the left-hand column. Don't write sentences, just key words (for example, "play tennis").

Topic	Me	My Partner
Something you couldn't do five years ago but can do now		
Something you used to do regularly five years ago but don't do now		
Something (or someone) you used to like five years ago, but don't like now		
Something (or someone) you never used to like five years ago, but like now		
A place you used to visit regularly five years ago, but don't visit these days		

Now work with your partner. Ask questions and complete the right-hand column with information about your partner. Try to get as much information as possible.

▶In Your Own Time

Turn to page 109 and complete the word list. Use your dictionary if you want to.
Use the CD at the back of your book and listen to the recordings in this unit again. The script for this unit is on pages 98, 99 and 100.

Unit 15 | I don't believe you!

▶Let's Start!

Work on your own. Place checks (✓) in the boxes to complete the questionnaire.

The Dating Game

■ When do young people usually start dating in your country?

☐ early teens   ☐ mid teens   ☐ late teens   ☐ early twenties

■ Who usually asks someone to go on a date?

☐ the girl   ☐ the boy   ☐ about 50-50

■ What do young people usually do on a first date?

☐ see a movie   ☐ go for a pizza   ☐ go for a drive   ☐ other

■ How long do the relationships usually last?

☐ a few weeks   ☐ a few months   ☐ about a year   ☐ two years or more

■ Why do young couples usually break up?

☐ boredom   ☐ another girl/boy   ☐ become too busy

Compare your answers with your partner.

Do you remember your very first boy/girlfriend? Tell your partner if you want to!

▶Before You Listen

Work with your partner. Look at the events in a typical girlfriend-boyfriend relationship.

Number them in order from _1_ (happens first) to _10_ (happens last). The first one is done for you.

.... they fall out

.... they have a great time

.... they break up

.... he fancies her

.... they start having problems

.... he asks her out

.... they start dating other people

.... they start going out

..1.... they meet

.... she agrees to a date

Compare your answers with another pair.

Do they have the same order or is it a little different?

Look at the pictures. Choose three expressions and write them next to the correct picture.

▸Let's Listen!

Listen to two conversations. Place a check (✓) in the box to show the best summary for each conversation.

Conversation 1: Karen's Story

☐ Jack and I didn't go out last night. We just met by chance at *Burger Heaven* and talked for a while.

☐ I saw Jack last night. He asked me out and said that you two were not dating anymore.

☐ Jack and I have been seeing each other for over a month. We are in love and I'm glad you found out.

Conversation 2: Jack's Story

☐ Karen and I didn't go out last night. We just met by chance at *Burger Heaven* and talked for a while.

☐ I met Karen by accident last night. She was a bit upset about her boyfriend and she suddenly started kissing me.

☐ I saw Karen last night but I didn't want to tell you about it. I thought you would misunderstand.

Check your answers with your partner.

▸Listen Again

CD Tracks: 78, 79

Listen to the conversations again. Number the events in the correct order. The first one is done for you.

Conversation 1: Karen's Story

.... Karen and Jack go to *Burger Heaven*
.... Karen tries to check with Diane
.... Jack tells Diane that he likes Karen
.... Jack asks Karen on a date
.... They kiss each other
___1___ Karen starts liking Jack
.... Jack and Diane break up

Conversation 2: Jack's Story

.... Karen kisses Jack
.... Karen calls Jack
.... Jack cancels his date with Diane
.... Karen tells Jack that she fancies him
___1___ Jack feels sick
.... Karen asks Jack to meet her
.... Jack feels uncomfortable

Listening Clinic One: A Final Look (1)

CD Track: 80

Work with your partner. Look at the dialogue. Circle places where you may find examples of the following points which you have studied in the *Listening Clinic* sections.

Lost Sounds   Helping Sounds   Weak Vowels

Mixed Sounds   Changing Sounds   Joined Sounds

A: Where were you last night, then?

B: I'm sorry, I had to go over some papers.

A: So why didn't you call me?

B: I tried to, but I got stuck in a meeting.

A: So how come Mary saw you in town?

B: Did she really?

A: With your assistant, Judy.

B: Look. I can explain, darling.

A: Would you stop playing with me for a minute!

Listen and check. Now say the dialogue together.

Practice!

Work with your partner. Tell your partner what you did yesterday. Include one small lie. Listen to your partner talking about yesterday. Try to find the lie.

Now Listen Back

CD Tracks: 78, 79

Listen to the conversations again and answer the questions.

■ Who do you think Diane believes?

....

■ Who do you believe?

....

Compare your answers with your partner.

Listen to the sentences. Circle the number of words in each sentence. Contractions (for example *she's*) count as two words.

1.   4   5   6
2.   4   5   6
3.   7   8   9
4.   6   7   8
5.   5   6   7
6.   1   2   3

Check your answers with your partner. Turn to page 101 and say the sentences.

Try It Out!

Work with your partner.

Roleplay One

Student A: You arranged to go out for lunch with your partner (Student B) yesterday but s/he did not come. You feel a bit annoyed. Some friends of yours saw Student B yesterday. Look at the pictures below. This is what they said Student B was doing. Call Student B and ask why they didn't come.

Student B: You didn't meet Student A yesterday. Think of a reason why. Make an *Alibi*. Think of an Alibi for the late morning, noon, the afternoon and the late afternoon. Student A will call you. Tell Student A your *Alibi*. Try to answer their questions.

Now change parts.

Roleplay Two

Student B: You arranged to study for a test with your partner, (Student A), yesterday but s/he did not come. You feel a bit annoyed. Some friends of yours saw Student A yesterday. Look at the pictures below. This is what they said Student A was doing. Call Student A and complain.

Student A: You didn't meet Student B last night. Think of a reason why. Make an *Alibi*. Think of an Alibi for yesterday evening between 7 and 10. Student B will call you. Tell Student B your *Alibi*. Try to answer their questions.

▸In Your Own Time

Turn to page 110 and complete the word list. Use your dictionary if you want to.
Use the CD at the back of your book and listen to the recordings in this unit again. The script for this unit is on pages 100 and 101.

Scripts

▶Unit 1: Good to see you again

Conversation 1

A: There she is.

B: Hello, Lynn. Hi Mari. Sorry I'm late.

C: That's okay, we haven't ordered yet. So, what's new?

B: Nothing much. Work's been really busy this week. That's why I had to rush to get here. How're things with you guys?

A: Same as usual. Overworked. Underpaid.

B: Yeah. Tell me about it. I've got this new boss. She's a nightmare. Works twenty five hours a day, and expects everybody else to do the same. I've been working till at least ten o'clock every night this week.

C: Well, it's Friday evening now, so you can relax a bit. Shall we get some food, then?

B: No. Let's get lots.

Conversation 2

Man: Hey, John. How's it going?

John: Good, thanks. How was your weekend?

Man: Ah, you know. Nothing special. You?

John: Uuhn, pretty quiet. I spent most of the time getting ready for this class. There's so much reading to do.

Man: Know what you mean. I was up till 4 a.m. finishing off that essay. I only got about four hours sleep last night.

John: Well, we've got about ten minutes before Professor Berry gets here. You want to get a coffee or something?

Man: Yeah, coffee sounds good.

Conversation 3

Joc.   Josh?

Josh: Joe! Wow. It's been ages. How've you been?

Joe: Just great. And you?

Josh: Yeah, great. Um, it's good to see you again. Ah… you remember Donna, don't you?

Joe: Sure. How have you been, Donna?

Donna: I'm fine, thanks. You're looking well, Joe.

Joe: Well-fed, maybe! But you haven't changed a bit.

Donna: Except for the hair.

Joe: No, it looks great.

Josh: It suits you, dear. Really!

Joe: So, Josh, what's new? Are you still working in New York?

Josh: Yeah, still in New York. But a, a different job from last time I saw you.

Joe: So you're not with the bank anymore?

Josh: No, I'm working for myself these days. Independent Financial Advisor.

Joe: Hard work, starting up on your own.

Josh: Yeah, but I'm enjoying it.

Joe: That's great! Good for you.

Conversation 4

Mark: Ken! Over here!

Ken: Hello, Mark. Good to see you.

Mark: You too. It's been a while, hasn't it? How was the flight?

Ken: Not too bad I suppose, just a bit long. I don't like flying.

Mark: Me neither. Still, you'll have plenty of time to rest over the next few days. Classes don't start till next Monday.

Ken: Sounds good.

Steven: Hello, Ken. Good to meet you.

Ken: Hi, Steven. You're Steven, right?

Steven: That's me.

Ken: You look just like your photo.

Steven: Oh, no! My brother didn't bore you with the family album, did he?

Ken: Not for long, anyway. You're at college now, aren't you?

Steven: That's right. I'm just home for spring break. I go back to Boston on Sunday.

Mark: Steve was at Oakfield High, too.

Steven: Yeah. I graduated last year. It's a good school. I'm sure you'll have a great time there. (Yeah). Especially with Mark to show you around.

Mark: Okay, Ken. Let's get you home and meet the rest of the family. The parking lot's this way. Oh, let me take that baggage cart.

Ken: No, it's okay.

Mark: No, really. You're the guest this time.

Ken: Okay then. Thanks.

⏵Unit 2: I've lost my rucksack

Conversation 1

Clerk: Midland Express. How can I help you?

Passenger: Hello. I traveled up to Birmingham on one of your services this morning, and I'm pretty sure I left my handbag on the bus.

Clerk: I see, madam. Um, which service were you traveling on?

Passenger: Oh, I don't know the number, but it was the London to Birmingham express, and it got in at about 10 o'clock.

Clerk: And could you describe the item for me, please?

Passenger: Yes, It's a small, shiny, black, plastic handbag (Uh-huh), with a short handstrap (Right) and a large silver-colored buckle (Mm). I was sitting near the…

Clerk: Yes, yes, it's okay, madam, we've got your bag. The er… driver handed it in.

Passenger: Oh, that's great. Now, what time can I come...

Conversation 2

Clerk: Yes, sir. How can I help you?

Passenger: It's, it's my briefcase. It's gone! It's, it's got all the documents for my meeting in Manchester and, oh hell…

Clerk: Alright sir. Alright. Just er… calm down a second. Now, er… if you could just start from the beginning, please. Er…, tell me exactly what happened.

Passenger: Right. Well, I was standing in line at that kiosk over there to get a sandwich to eat on the train (Right), and I put my briefcase down on the floor beside me while I took out some money to pay the cashier (Okay)… ten seconds later I went to pick it up, and, and it's gone.

Clerk: Oh, okay. And what does it look like, sir?

Passenger: Look like? It's, it's just an ordinary briefcase. Large, brown, leather... Oh, and it, it has my initials, L.R.S., monogrammed on it.

Clerk: Right sir. And when did you say you...?

Conversation 3

A: Excuse me.

B: Yeah?

A: You didn't see someone pick up a blue sports bag, did you?

B: Sorry.

A: Yeah, a big, blue, nylon sports bag with a big, white *Adidas* logo on the side.

B: I said *no*.

A: I only put it down for a moment when I went into the restroom. Then I came out and...

B: I can't help you.

A: I don't believe it! I had a brand new racket in there and ten new balls and a...

B: Well, these are public courts, pal. Anyone can walk in here. You should be more careful.

Conversation 4

Clerk: Yes, sir?

Passenger: Hi there. I'm trying to find my suitcase. Ah, I came in on flight AL272 from Rome.

Clerk: Okay.

Passenger: But I got delayed at Immigration.

Clerk: I see, sir.

Passenger: It looks like the baggage claim for that flight's closed already.

Clerk: That's right, sir. We took the last bags off the carousel about ten minutes ago.

Passenger: Ah, well, where can I pick up my suitcase?

Clerk: We should have it here, sir.

Passenger: Great. Erm... it's a large purple suitcase, er... hard shell *Samsonite*, and it's got a rainbow-colored elastic strap wrapped around it. You can't miss it.

Clerk: Okay, sir. And do you have your baggage claim slip? It should be attached to your ticket.

Passenger: Oh, ah yes... hang on a sec. Here you are.

Clerk: Okay, thank you, sir. If you'll just wait here a moment, I'll er... get your suitcase.

Unit 3: I'd like you to meet my brother

Conversation 1

Kerry: Oh, look. There's Bob Hatton. Quick.

Bob: Kerry. Hi, how's it going?

Kerry: Hey, Bob. Yeah, everything's fine. So Bob, say hello to Yumi.

Bob: Hi, Yumi.

Yumi: Hi, Bob.

Kerry: Yumi's here from Japan on a one-year exchange program. I'm her mentor for this semester.

Bob: Great... So, where in Japan, Yumi?

Yumi: I'm from Yokohama.

Bob: Ah, well... *hajime mashite*.

Yumi: Hajime mashite.... So, you speak Japanese?

Bob: I know about ten words of Japanese. You just heard two of them. Want to hear the others?

Yumi: Ah, well...

Bob: *Sushi, tempura, judo, karate...*

Kerry: Take no notice of him, Yumi. He's always like this. (*Karaoke, hibachi, sumo, sayonara, konichiwa*)

Yumi: You mean he's always a—what's the word—jerk?

Conversation 2

Tyler McCoy: Professor Wylie?

Professor Wylie: Ah, yes?

Tyler McCoy: We haven't met before. Er... my name's Tyler McCoy. I'm a colleague of Mike Hardy's at Green Lake College.

Professor Wylie: Oh right. Well, good to meet you, Tyler. How is Mike these days? It must be over a year now since I saw him last.

Tyler McCoy: Yeah, Mike's fine. When he heard I was coming to this conference, he said I should definitely come and hear you speak and I'm glad he did. It was really interesting.

Professor Wylie: Well, thank you very much.

Tyler McCoy:	Actually, professor, there was something I wanted to ask you…. Erm, something you mentioned in your talk.
Professor Wylie:	Sure, and please no more 'Professor'. It makes me feel old. The name's Ron.
Tyler McCoy:	Okay. Well, er... Ron, it was about that point you made about fractal parsing of the…

Conversation 3

Miss Smith:	Yes? Who is it?… Okay, okay. I'm coming! Yes?
Lynn Murray:	Hi, there. I just moved in next door. I thought I'd come round and say "hello". I'm Lynn Murray. Please call me Lynn. Er... and you are...?
Miss Smith:	The name's Smith.
Lynn Murray:	Uh… right. Well, it's nice to meet you, Mrs. Smith.
Miss Smith:	That's Miss Smith, if you don't mind.
Lynn Murray:	Miss Smith. Right. And this is little baby James. I'm afraid he's too young to say hello. He's just ten months now.
Miss Smith:	A baby, hm? Well, Mrs. Murray, I hope you'll keep him quiet. I hate noisy neighbors.
Lynn Murray:	Oh, don't worry. James won't be living here. He's my nephew. I'm just babysitting him today for my sister. So it's Miss Murray actually.
Miss Smith:	Hmph!

Conversation 4

Mr. Burns:	Hello John. Remember me?
John:	Mr. Burns! Great to see you! I'm really glad you could make it.
Mr. Burns:	Glad to be invited. And congratulations!
John:	Thanks.
Mr. Burns:	You remember my wife Angela, don't you?
John:	Actually we never met, though I'm sure we talked on the phone once or twice.
Mrs. Burns:	Several times. It's good to meet you at last, John.
John:	You too, Mrs. Burns.
Mrs. Burns:	So, aren't you going to introduce us to your beautiful bride?
John:	Oh yeah, I'm sorry. Mr. and Mrs. Burns, this is my lovely wife, Kathy.
Kathy:	Hello. Nice to meet you both.
John:	Mr. Burns was my piano teacher for three years. Without him I'd never have made it into music school.
Mr. Burns:	John's being too modest. He always had the talent. And now he's a professional musician.
John:	Well, hotel lounges and the occasional jazz club. It's not very glamorous.
Mrs. Burns:	But at least you're working at something you love. Your parents must be very proud of you.
John:	Yeah, I guess so.
Mr. Burns:	Talking of your parents, how are they these days?

| | John: | They're fine. They're around here somewhere. Why don't I take you to find them? I'm sure they'd love to see you again. |

John: They're fine. They're around here somewhere. Why don't I take you to find them? I'm sure they'd love to see you again.

Mr. Burns: Yes. That'd be great.

Mrs. Burns: Yes, lovely. I've always wanted to meet your parents.

John: Okay. Let's go.

Unit 4: Final Call for Flight EA42

Announcement 1

North American Airways Flight NA115 to Las Vegas will begin boarding through Gate 43 at 11:15 a.m. The new departure time for this flight is 11:45 a.m. We apologize for the delayed departure. This is due to the late arrival of a connecting flight.

Announcement 2

We would like to remind all passengers not to leave suitcases or other luggage items unattended at any time. Unattended luggage will be removed immediately by the police and will be destroyed. We thank you for your cooperation.

Announcement 3

Passenger Singh, travelling on East Asian Airways Flight EA42 to Hanoi. Please go to the East Asian Airways Jasmine Lounge in the International Departures area. Passenger Singh.

Announcement 4

Pan Pacific Airways Flight 4 to Hong Kong is now ready to begin boarding through Gate 40. We will begin boarding passengers with small children, business class passengers, and economy class passengers in rows 41 through 54. Please check your seat allocation before presenting your boarding pass.

Unit 7: Try It Out! Student A

Look at the table below. You are missing information about Britain. Your partner has this information. Ask your partner questions to complete the table. Write all numbers as figures: for example, 350,000.

	Japan	Britain
Population:	127,000,000	....
Size (in square kilometers):	377,000	....
Exports per year (in US dollars):	400,000,000,000	....
Main Airport:	Tokyo Narita Airport	....
Number of passengers per year:	25,000,000	....

Look at the table. Use the table to answer your partner's questions about Japan.

Unit 5: It's a great deal!

Music Today magazine called them "the most original new band of the new century." *Rock Weekly* called the album "a spell-binding collection of beautifully-crafted tunes." "No Deposit," the new album from The Empties. Hear it before you buy it at www.breakingrecords.com.

Commercial 2

A: Jane! You look fantastic! And that dress! Why, it can't be more than a size 10.

B: Size 8 actually. I lost ten kilos in the last two weeks. And I feel great too.

A: Ten kilos! That's amazing! But it must have been really hard work.

B: Not at all. It was really easy. Thanks to Fatticide.

A: Fatticide?

B: Yes, Fatticide Body Cream. Just rub it on every night before bedtime, and while you're asleep the fat just melts away. No need for painful exercise or boring diets. Eat what you like and still lose weight.

A: Sounds great! So where do I get my Fatticide?

B: Just dial 0800-88-8888 with your credit card information.

C: Fatticide. Call now. 0800-88-8888. For a slimmer you.

Commercial 3

Hi, folks. This is Big Bill Fenderbender, and I wanna welcome y'all to Big Bill's Auto Heaven's Massive Labor Day Clearout. Almost a hundred low-mileage Fords, Mazdas and Chevies must be sold this weekend. You won't find a better deal anywhere. We have the widest range, the best finance deals, and the friendliest service. Big Bill's Auto Heaven, located in Auto Mall Parkway, just off I-84 in Sunnydale. For really great cars at really great prices, come on down to Big Bill's Auto Heaven. A great day out for your whole family.

Commercial 4

A: Hi, Greg. You look a bit fed-up. What's up?

B: Oh, hi, Mike. I just spent a whole morning on my computer trying to download a piece of software from the Internet. First, I couldn't get through to my ISP—the lines are always really busy on a Monday morning—and then when I did get connected the file just took forever to download. No wonder they call it World Wide Wait.

A: You should do what I did. Switch to Cosmo Cable. The Internet connection is always on, so you don't have to worry about busy phone lines, and downloads are lightning fast, 30 times faster than a dial-up modem.

B: Yeah, but it's really expensive, right?

A: Wrong. I'm getting unlimited Internet access from Cosmo Cable for just $29.95 a month. That's five dollars a month less than I was paying for my old dial-up ISP. And now I don't have to worry about telephone charges.

B: Yes. But, what about installation? It's always expensive to get cable put into your house, isnt it?

A: Well, that's another great deal. Cosmo Cable are offering free installation until the end of this month, so if you sign up now you can save over a hundred dollars.

B: Wow! So what do I do?

A: Phone 1-800-555-5543. That's 1-800-555-5543 or sign up online at www.cosmocable.com.

C: Cosmo Cable. It's faster. It's cheaper. It's more reliable. Isn't it time you got connected?

Unit 6: That's not good enough

Conversation 1

Clerk: Housekeeping. Good evening. How can I help you?

Guest: Ah, hi there. This is room 321. Ah... I, I can't get the TV to work.

Clerk: I see, sir. Have you followed the instructions on the card?

Guest: Ah, ah...what card?

Clerk: There should be a card on top of the TV set. It has instructions on how to use the remote control, select movies and other services.

Guest: There's no card in this room. Nothing on the TV, anyway.

Clerk: Oh, I'm terribly sorry, sir. We'll send someone to your room right away.

Guest: Okay. Thanks.

Conversation 2

Clerk: Good evening. Room Service. How may we help you?

Ms. Harrison: Yeah. This is room 1249. I ordered some food half an hour ago, and it still hasn't arrived.

Unit 14: Practice! Student A

Your are missing some information in the table below. Ask your partner questions to complete the table.

	15 YEARS AGO	NOW
Name:	Billy Angel	....
Occupation:	....	Taxi Driver
Salary:	$800,000 a year	....
Home:	....	3-bedroom house in Cleveland, Ohio

Your partner is missing different information. Use information in the table to answer your partner's questions.

Clerk:	Yes ma'am. Sorry for the delay. We've had a sudden rush of orders during the last hour. Room 1249, Ms. Harrison?
Ms. Harrison:	That's right.
Clerk:	We're working on your order right now, and we'll be delivering it soon.
Ms. Harrison:	Soon? How soon is "soon"?
Clerk:	I would say another fifteen to twenty minutes, ma'am.
Ms. Harrison:	Twenty minutes? You mean it takes you people an hour to get a hamburger together?
Clerk:	As I just explained, ma'am, we've had...
Ms. Harrison:	Oh, just forget it. I'll go out and get something.
Clerk:	It really won't take much longer, Ms. Harrison. I'm sure the cook can...
Ms. Harrison:	I said forget it. Goodnight.

Conversation 3

Clerk: Reception. How can I help you?

Guest: Yeah. I phoned you about ten minutes ago to tell you I was ready to check out and to ask for a bellhop to come for my bags, but no-one's come yet.

Clerk: Oh, I er.. um...

Guest: Yeah, well, it, it's just I'm worried, I'm going to be late for my flight.

Clerk: I see, sir. It's, um room 842, isn't it?

Guest: That's right, yeah.

Clerk: Yes, we're very sorry to have kept you waiting. Er... it's just we've had a rather large party of, uh, conventioneers all checking out together (I see), and uh, we've been rather stretched down here, so... But there is a bellhop on his way to your room right now, sir.

Guest: Okay. It, it's just that I'm worried about my flight.

Clerk: I understand, sir, yes. Erm... there should be someone with you any moment now, and er... check out will only take a moment. Erm... the shuttle to the airport leaves on the hour and that'll get you to the airport in er... fifteen minutes.

Guest: Oh, great. Okay. Well, thanks a lot, eh.

Clerk: Well, you're quite welcome, sir.

Conversation 4

Clerk:	Good morning, sir.
Mr. Campbell:	Hi there. We have a reservation. The name's Campbell.
Clerk:	One moment, please, Mr. Campbell... Yes, here we are. Mr. and Mrs. Campbell.
Mr. Campbell:	That's right.
Clerk:	We have you down for a five-night stay. Is that right?
Mr. Campbell:	Yes, that's right.
Clerk:	Okay, Mr. Campbell. Your room number is 1208. On the 12th floor. A twin room, garden view...
Mr. Campbell:	Whoa whoa, wait, wait a minute. That's not what I reserved actually. I specifically requested a suite with an ocean view. Here... Look... Here's a copy of

	your confirmation email, see? "25th to 30th—five nights—suite—ocean view."
Clerk:	Yes, I see. Well, I'm terribly sorry, sir, uh, let me see what I can do... Uh, okay, um... let's see... Uh, we do have one ocean view room available (Mm-hm). It's a corner room on the 15th floor (Mm-hm), so it has an excellent ocean view (Mm-hm), but I'm afraid it's a twin-bed room...
Mr. Campbell:	Twin? This is our honeymoon. We don't want a twin.
Clerk:	I'm really sorry, Mr. Campbell, but the hotel is fully booked this week. It's all we have left.
Mr. Campbell:	No. That's not good enough. You confirmed this reservation two months ago. I want the room I requested (Yes). The room you agreed to provide.
Clerk:	Yes, well, I understand how you...
Mr. Campbell:	Just get me the manager, will you?
Clerk:	Oh, oh, er... yeah, of course, Mr. Campbell. If you'll just wait here a moment, I'll try to find him for you.
Mr. Campbell:	Don't try. Find him.

Listening Clinic 2

1. This hamburger's completely cold.
2. I've never eaten such terrible food.
3. We'll send someone immediately.
4. There's a spider in my soup.
5. I'm terribly sorry about that.
6. I'd like to apologize for everything.

Unit 7: Did you see the paper?

Conversation 1

A: What about sales volume?

B: Well, considering the economy's not doing well, I think the figures have been pretty good. Sales in Europe are up 2% on last year, and in the US they're up 1%.

A: What about Asia?

B: Not so good, I'm afraid. Sales volume is down 7% compared to last year. The only good news is that our *Slingshot* disposable camera is selling very strongly in all Asian markets. In the three years since it was launched we've had total sales of eight million units.

A: That's good. Really good. I wish we had a few more products like that.

Conversation 2

Tour Guide:	So... everyone, gather round, please. Okay, now this is Tokyo station. From the outside, it's pretty impressive, isn't it?
Mrs. Lewis:	Well, this Marunouchi entrance—darling look here—it's one of the most famous buildings in Tokyo. It's modeled after the old central station in Amsterdam.
Mr. Lewis:	Yes, dear. Very interesting.

Tour Guide:	That's right, Mrs. Lewis. But I am sure that Amsterdam station never gets as busy as this.
Mrs. Lewis:	It says here about eight hundred thousand people use this station every day.
Tour Guide:	Very good, Mrs. Lewis. Eight hundred thousand. And it looks like they're all here now.
Mrs. Lewis:	But according to this, Shinjuku Station is twice as busy. Is that right, Ms. Saito?

Conversation 3

| Interviewer: | Professor Lowe. In your latest book, *Towards Tomorrow*, you say that population control will be the biggest challenge facing the world in the 21st century. Why is that? |
| Professor Lowe: | Well, in terms of population growth, I think there's both good news and bad news. The good news is that the world's population will probably reach its peak in the middle of the 21st century, and after that it will level off, maybe even fall a little. The bad news is that by the year 2050 there'll probably be more than eight billion people living on this planet, that's 25% more than we have today, so obviously we need to start thinking right now about how we are going to deal with this huge increase, all the extra people. |

Conversation 4

A:	Did you see this on the sports page?
B:	See what?
A:	Manchester United have just paid eighty million US dollars for a new striker.
B:	Wow!
A:	Listen. "Italian striker Basil Panini has become the world's most expensive soccer player in an eighty-million-dollar move from *Roma* to *Manchester United*."
B:	Eighty million?
A:	Yeah. "The 22-year-old international has signed a five-year contract worth an estimated seven million US dollars a year."
B:	Wow!
A:	"With a weekly salary of over one hundred and thirty thousand US dollars, Panini will become the highest-paid player in world of soccer."
B:	One hundred and thirty thousand a week! That's more than twice what I earn in a whole year!
A:	And that's just his basic salary. It says here that with bonuses and advertising contracts he'll probably make over seventy million dollars during the five years of his contract.
B:	I knew it was a big mistake.
A:	What was a big mistake?
B:	Studying hard at school and going to university. I should've spent more time playing soccer instead of doing homework.
A:	Yeah. Me too.

Johnny:	Okay. Let's go over the plan one more time.
Billy:	But Johnny, we've been over it, over and over...
Johnny:	And now we're going over it again. You got a problem with that, Billy Boy?
Billy:	No, Uncle Johnny, I was just...
Johnny:	Right. Algernon. Where are you and your guys going to be?
Algernon:	We'll be across from the bank.
Johnny:	Time?
Algernon:	8:45. We start setting up. We'll probably get started at around 9:15.
Johnny:	Not good enough.
Algernon:	Okay, 9:15. We start drilling and making noise at 9:15.
Johnny:	Bob?
Bob:	8:00 a.m. I'm having coffee and donuts across the street.
Billy:	Coffee and donuts!
Bob:	Hey, I'm going to be dressed as a cop, right?
Johnny:	Enough. Come on. What are you doing, Bob?
Bob:	Watching the bank.
Johnny:	No!
Bob:	The subway entrance. And the side street. You're watching the bank, boss. From the bus stop on the corner.
Johnny:	Billy and Benny G?
Billy:	We're parked in the street next to the bank. I've got car trouble and, ah, Benny G here's helping me.
Johnny:	Time?
Benny G:	9:20.

Unit 7: Try It Out! Student B

Look at the table below. Your partner is missing information about Britain. Use the table to answer your partner's questions.

	Japan	Britain
Population:	....	60,000,000
Size (in square kilometers):	....	243,000
Exports per year (in US dollars):	....	270,000,000,000
Main Airport:	....	London Heathrow
Number of passengers per year:	....	64,000,000

Look at the table. You are missing information about Japan. Ask your partner questions to complete the table. Write all numbers as figures: for example, 350,000.

Johnny: Okay. Routines? Actions?

Algernon: The manager will probably be the first to arrive. He drives in, makes a left at the coffee shop and a right down the side street. Parks in the lot behind the bank. He enters the bank from the side entrance. He'll probably arrive between 8:00 and 8:15.

Johnny: Staff?

Benny G: The tellers arrive a bit later. Probably around 8:40.

Johnny: Around? Not good enough, Benny G.

Benny G: Okay, okay. Between 8:30 and 8:45, Johnny. They might go in through the side entrance if it's raining, but'll probably go in through the main doors. The manager lets them in.

Johnny: Security. Billy?

Billy: One old guy. Jenkins. He'll probably get there between 8:55 and 9:05. He's always the last to arrive. Comes by bus. Gets off and uh, probably'll walk down the street and pick up a sandwich at the bakery. Crosses the road and goes inside. Side entrance. The bank opens at 9:30.

Johnny: So what do we do? Bob.

Bob: As soon as I see the manager start to open the doors, I leave the coffee shop and walk into the bank. Behind you boss. 9:32. We do the job.

Johnny: Drivers?

Benny G: The job will probably take between 12 and 15 minutes. We're going to start our engines at 9:40. Not before.

Billy: 'coz we don't want to look too suspicious.

Bob: Johnny, I really think we're going to need guns.

Johnny: No. No guns. We won't need them. The folks in the bank, they're going to be scared. Real scared. And you might have another little accident, Bob. Remember? Okay. Let's go over it one more time. 'Til we get it right. Benny G? Where are you guys going to be?

Unit 9: How are we feeling today?

Conversation 1

Doctor: Hmm… That looks painful. What happened?

Patient: I fell off my bike.

Doctor: Hmm. Could you try to move it for me? … Um, good. Now up and down…Okay. Now try to move your fingers, one at a time.

Patient: Like this?

Doctor: Mm-hm, Fine…Now, does it hurt when I do this?

Patient: Ah! Yeah, a little bit, yeah.

Doctor: Hmm. And how about this?

Patient: Aah!

Doctor: Oh, sorry….Well, I don't think it's broken. It's probably just a bad sprain, but it'll be swollen and painful for at least a week or two. I'm going to send you for an X-ray, just to make sure.

Conversation 2

Doctor: Okay. Let's have a look at her.
Mother: Uh-huh.
Doctor: Could you take off her diaper?
Mother: Okay.
Doctor: Ah, yes, I see…Well, it's very uncomfortable for the baby and it certainly explains why she's been crying more than usual (Oh). But this kind of rash is very common.
Mother: Uh-huh.
Doctor: A baby's skin is extremely sensitive. Tell me, have you changed brands for any of your baby products recently?
Mother: Ah, like you mean…
Doctor: You know, diapers, soap, anything like that?
Mother: Er…well, I did start using a different baby powder a couple of weeks ago.
Doctor: Mm… well, maybe you should try going back to the old one.
Mother: Okay.
Doctor: And I'll give you some cream to put on her each time you change the diaper. That should clear up the spots and stop the itching.
Mother: Oh, thank you, doctor. You know I was so worried because I thought that….

Conversation 3

Doctor: So how long have you been having this pain?
Patient: About two weeks, doctor.

Unit 14: Practice! Student B

Your partner is missing some information in the table below. You have this information. Use the table to answer your partner's questions.

	15 YEARS AGO	NOW
Name:	....	Bill Anderson
Occupation:	Teenage Pop Idol	....
Salary:	....	$25,000 a year
Home:	12-bedroom house in Beverly Hills	....

Now, ask your partner questions to complete your missing information.

Doctor: And have you had this kind of pain before?

Patient: No, never. That's why I'm so worried. Am I... am I going to have a heart attack, doctor?

Doctor: Don't worry, Mr. Simpson. Most chest pains have nothing to do with heart problems. It's more likely indigestion or a food allergy. But let's have a listen to your heart anyway. Could you unbutton your shirt for me, please?

Conversation 4

Doctor:	Now Mrs. Jones, if you could just step up onto the scales... Hmm. It seems you've put on quite a bit since last month. Have you been following the diet sheet I gave you?
Mrs. Jones:	Yes, doctor... Well, most of the time I have. But I do get really hungry late in the evening sometimes, and I just have to have an extra snack before bedtime.
Doctor:	Late night snacks, huh? What kind of snacks?
Mrs. Jones:	Cookies usually. And just a small packet... usually.
Doctor:	Right. And what about exercise? Have you been exercising properly?
Mrs. Jones:	Well, I wanted to, but the weather's been so bad these last few weeks...
Doctor:	Mrs. Jones, you're at least 40 kilos overweight, and it's seriously damaging your health. You also have dangerously high blood pressure. You must follow the diet sheet exactly every day. No snacks, and no food at all after 7 p.m. And you really must try to exercise a little bit every day.

▶Unit 10: Could you give me a hand?

Conversation 1

Dad: Sean, will you hurry up and eat properly? You're just moving those peas around your plate.

Sean: I don't like peas. Why do you always give them to me? You know I don't like them.

Dad: You don't like any vegetables. But you've got to eat some.

Sean: Why?

Dad: You know why. Now hurry up and eat.

Sean: Can I have some ice cream?

Dad: No. Not until you finish those peas.

Sean: I hate peas.

Conversation 2

Mom:	Okay, Matthew. Time for bed.
Matthew:	But Mom, *Murder Squad* is starting in five minutes. Can't I stay up?!
Mom:	No. It's nine o'clock and you've got school tomorrow. Now go on.
Matthew:	It's not fair. You let Kelly stay up till ten.
Mom:	Kelly's two years older than you. Now get upstairs, and don't forget to brush your teeth.
Matthew:	Can I tape it and watch it tomorrow?
Mom:	No, you can't. I've told you before. I don't want you watching *Murder Squad*. It's not

	a program for kids. It's too violent. Now go to bed.
Matthew:	But Jason's mom lets him watch it.
Mom:	I don't care what Jason's mom does. I won't tell you again. Get upstairs, brush your teeth, and go to bed.
Matthew:	Aw. It's not fair.

Conversation 3

Son: Dad?

Dad: Yep?

Son: Do you remember I told you I was thinking of asking Cindy Johnson for a date?

Dad: Yeah, I remember.

Son: Well, I did. And she said yes.

Dad: Well, good for you, son.

Son: Yeah it's great, isn't it? I'm taking her out on Sunday, only I'm a bit short of cash. Do you think you could lend me twenty dollars till I get paid next week?

Dad: Umm, yeah okay. But I want it back on pay day. Or I can take it off your allowance if you like.

Son: Whatever. Thanks, Dad.

Conversation 4

Mom: Claire. How many times do I have to tell you, get off the phone. I'm expecting a call.

Claire: Yeah, yeah… Listen Susie, gotta go. I'll call you back in a few minutes. Bye… Sorry about that. It was Susie. Her and Beth are going to the mall this afternoon. Is it okay if I go?

Mom: Have you cleaned your room?

Claire: No, not yet, but I can do that tomorrow.

Mom: No, you'll do it today, like we agreed.

Claire: Oh, okay then. So can I go to the mall after I clean my room?

Mom: What about your homework?

Claire: Tomorrow's Sunday. I can do my homework tomorrow.

Mom: No you can't. Have you forgotten? We're going to Grandma's tomorrow. We'll be there all day.

Claire: Oh no, how boring.

Mom: So you've got a busy day today, young lady. Better get started on your room.

Unit 11: This is the six o'clock news

Good evening. You're listening to Asia FM. This is Martin Ford with the news headlines for this hour.

In Okinawa, Japan, homeowners and businesses are continuing their efforts to clean up the damage caused by Typhoon Number 17, which hit the island yesterday. Winds of more than 160 kilometers per hour knocked down trees, overturned cars and destroyed more than 200 homes.

More than 700 millimeters of rain fell in twenty-four hours, causing heavy flooding. In the main city of Naha, rising flood waters have forced several hundred people to leave their homes. The Japanese government has sent 500 emergency relief workers from Tokyo to help in the rescue and recovery efforts.

Share prices on the New York Stock Exchange have fallen sharply following yesterday's decision to raise US interest rates by one percentage point. American investors appear to be worried that higher interest rates will make the US dollar stronger. And a stronger dollar makes doing business more difficult for American companies who export to European and Asian markets.

Eight-year-old kidnap victim Jenny Lin has been returned safely to her family. The Hong Kong schoolgirl was rescued by police yesterday at an apartment in Kowloon, three days after she disappeared on her way to school. Police have arrested the owner of the apartment. Jenny's father said that his daughter was unharmed and very glad to be home. He thanked the police for their good work in finding Jenny so soon and returning her safely to the family.

And finally, in sports, French teenager Marie Duval has become the youngest-ever winner of a professional tennis tournament by winning the ladies singles title at the Honolulu Open tournament in Hawaii. Duval, who celebrated her 13th birthday just two weeks ago, came back from losing the first set in the final to beat American Mary Wilson 5-7, 6-4, 6-2.

Unit 12: Can I take a message?

Conversation 1

Man: Good morning. Happy House.

Keiji: Uh, good morning. Can I speak to Leah Green, please?

Man: Leah? Um, I think she's gone out. Let me just check. Um, could I ask who's calling?

Keiji: Keiji, Keiji Makino.

Man: Okay, let me just check. Yeah, Keiji. She went out about an hour ago. I'm sorry but I don't really know when she'll be back. Uh… Can I take a message or, uh, get her to call you?

Keiji: Er, no. It's not urgent. Could you just tell her that I called and that I'll call again tomorrow?

Man: Okay. I'll do that.

Keiji: Thanks. Bye.

Man: Goodbye.

Conversation 2

Receptionist: Good morning. Atangan Associates. How can I help you?

Maria: Good morning. Could I speak to Ben Atangan, please?

Receptionist: I'm afraid Mr. Atangan's with a client at the moment. May I take a message?

Maria: Yes, please. This is his cousin, Maria…

Receptionist: Oh yes, from the Philippines… He said you were arriving this week. You're in town?

Maria:	Yes. I just got in this morning.
Receptionist:	Oh great! Ben, um, Mr. Atangan's been waiting for your call. He's really been looking forward to your visit. I know he'll want to speak to you as soon as he's done. How can he reach you?
Maria:	Well, I'm going to my *tita's*, um, my Auntie Flora's, for lunch. He should have the number there but I'll give it to you anyway. It's 474-6561.
Receptionist:	474-6561?
Maria:	Yes.
Receptionist:	Okay. I'll get him to call you as soon as he's free.
Maria:	Thanks. Goodbye.
Receptionist:	Bye-bye. And nice talking with you. Welcome to LA.
Maria:	Thanks. Bye.

Conversation 3

Anita:	Yardley Catering. Good morning.
Tom Shepherd:	Hello. Anita? This is Tom Shepherd. Is Delila there?
Anita:	Oh, hello, Mr. Shepherd. I'm sorry, she's out on a job at the moment. You could try her on her cell phone. Shall I give you the number?
Tom Shepherd:	It's okay. I've got the number. Okay, I'll do that. Thanks. Bye.

Conversation 4

Jason:	Fairweather Landscapes, Jason speaking. How can I help you?
Mr. Fern:	Hello, ah, I'd like to speak to Mr. Fairweather, please.
Jason:	Ah, Mr. Fairweather. I'm afraid he's in a meeting at the moment. Can I ask who's calling?
Mr. Fern:	Yes. This is Keith Fern from Auburn Garden Center. Ah, I want to arrange a meeting with Mr. Fairweather, so…
Jason:	Um, shall I get him to call you back?
Mr. Fern:	Yes…. Oh, no, no…I'm going to be tied up myself for the rest of the day. Could you ask him to email me? He's got the address.
Jason:	Okay, it's about your meeting…?
Mr. Fern:	Yes. Ah, if you could ask him to suggest a few possible times for next week.
Jason:	Okay. I'll give him the message.
Mr. Fern:	Thanks. Oh, and by the way, could you tell him I can't make Wednesday next week, but any other day may be okay.
Jason:	Sure. I'll tell him that. And it's Mr. Fern, yeah?
Mr. Fern:	Yes. F-E-R-N.
Jason:	Okay then.
Mr. Fern:	Thanks a lot then. Bye.
Jason:	Bye.

Unit 13: How do you work this?

Conversation 1

A: How do I get this thing to work then?

B: Have you put the dish in?

A: Yeah. It's ready to go. I just don't know how to make it start.

B: Okay. Well, how long does the recipe say?

A: Hang on... ahh... eight minutes at 500 watts, seven minutes at 600 watts.

B: Alright. Well, this is 600 watts, so put the time in on the number pad. Seven... zero... zero.

A: Okay.

B: Then press the start button. And that's it.

A: Well, that was pretty painless.

B: Don't speak too soon. We haven't tasted it yet.

Conversation 2

A: So do you want to dub the whole album?

B: Well, that's easier, isn't it?

A: Yeah, it's, er... much easier.

B: Okay, let's do that then.

A: Alright. So, press the open/close button and put the CD in Tray One.

B: Yeah.

A: Good. Now, ah, press the button again (Mm-hmm) and close the tray (Okay). Okay, now, put the blank MD in the MD slot (Uh-huh). No, no, not (Oh) like that. No. No. (Oh, oh, okay) You see that arrow on the side there?

B: Yeah.

A: Yeah. That's got to go in first.

B: What? You mean like, like this?

A: Yeah, that's right. Good, Now, now press the button with the red dot on it.

B: Well, it's flashing. Is that it?

A: Uh, yeah, that's it. Yeah.

B: Okay... But do I need to adjust the volume level?

A: Only if you want to listen to it now. Do you, do you want to do it now?

B: No, that's okay.

A: Well, then the recording level's automatic.

B: Oh, okay.

Conversation 3

A: So how do I get rid of it?

B: Easy. Just right click on the program icon, scroll down the menu list, click delete, click okay in the dialogue box, and the icon should disappear from the desktop.

A: Come on! I can't remember all that! Please, start again. And this time, step by step, and slowly!

A: Okay. Now, this machine has G-code, which makes things a lot easier.

B: Good. I'm useless with these machines.

A: Oh, don't worry. It's easy to remember. Power's on, right?

B: Yeah.

A: Okay. So first you have to put in the tape.

B: Yeah, I've done that. There's a new one in there ready to go.

A: Good. Ah, now take the remote control and press the *program* button.

B: Okay.

A: Now press the *G-code* button.

B: This one?

A: Yeah, that's it. Now enter the program code.

B: Program code?

A: Oh yeah, sorry, I should have explained before. Every program has a number code (Uh-huh). Ah... it tells the machine what time and channel to record.

B: Okay.

A: The codes are here in the TV guide, next to the program name.

B: Oh.

A: Right. So you need to enter... hang on a minute... 94533.

B: 9-4-5-3-3

A: That's it. Then you press the *send* button and that sends the information from the remote control to the machine.

B: *Send*. Okay.

A: And then press the *timer set* button. When that little red clock icon lights up, the timer is on and it's all done.

B: Well, that's a whole lot easier than my old machine. Even I should be able to remember that.

▶Unit 14: Things have changed

A: Still smoking? Don't you realize how bad that is for your health?

B: Look, I enjoy it. And you can't talk. I can remember when you used to, you used to get through what... a pack a day, a pack a day.

A: Yeah, yeah, yeah, but that was before (Before). And I haven't touched, I haven't touched a cigarette for almost a year now.

B; Oh, yes, you have.

A: I have not. And I'll tell you what (What)... I feel so much better for it (Well, good for you, mate). I used have a really bad cough all the time.

B: You still cough. You still cough.

A: No, that's gone now (Well). And I used to feel really tired in the morning.

B: You're still tired in the mornings.

A: No, I'm not. Now I feel really fresh when I get up (Yeah). It's great.

B: So, so if I want to be this Superman like you, you, I've got to quit too, right?
A: Right you are.
B: Wrong.

A: The place looks so different.
B: Well, you've been away a long time. What is it… ten years?
A: Twelve years.
B: It's a long time.
A: I know, but even so, that open space over there. That used to be the movie theater, didn't it?
B: The Odeon? It was knocked down last year.
A: The Odeon, yeah. I remember when we used to go there on Saturday mornings. The kids shows there. *Batman*, *Tom and Jerry*, the old cartoons.
B: Yeah.
A: I've got some happy memories of that place.
B: Well, you should have seen it a few years ago. It was dirty, the seats were old, nobody wanted to go there anymore.
A: Really?
B: Yeah, they're building a big new one on the other side of town now. Ten screens, armchair seats, top-class sound system.
A: Wow.
B: Yeah, it's going to be much better.
A: Well, that's progress, I guess.
B: I suppose it is.

Conversation 3

A: How many times do I have to say it? I'm sorry. I've been so busy recently, I just forgot.
B: Yeah, well I can't believe that you'd forget my birthday. What's happened to you, Jim? You used to be so romantic. When we first started dating you were always buying me presents —flowers, chocolates, jewelry. Now you can't even remember my birthday.
A: I know. Look, I'm sorry. It's just that…
B: And we never do anything interesting anymore, do we? We used to go to restaurants, parties, clubs. Now all you want to do is stay home and watch videos. You never used to be so, so… so boring.
A: And you never used to complain so much about everything. Everything I do these days is wrong What about you, then? You're not perfect. Have you looked in the mirror recently? You used to be so slim. Now look at you. When we first met, you were a size 10. What's your dress size these days? 14? 16? Hmph. Buy you chocolates? You've got to be kidding!
B: Are you saying I'm, I'm I'm fat?
A: I'm saying I'm sick of these stupid arguments. I'm going home.

Unit 15: I don't believe you!

Conversation 1

Karen: Diane. How's things?

Diane: Karen. Did you have a good time last night?

Karen: What do you mean?

Diane: You look a bit tired. I guess that's because you spent all last night with my boyfriend.

Karen: What are you talking about?

Diane: You know exactly what I'm talking about. You and Jack. Last night. Outside the Burger Heaven.

Karen: Wait a minute, Diane. You've got this all wrong.

Diane: You can't deny it, Karen. Mary saw you. She told me this morning. He's quite a kisser, isn't he?

Karen: No, listen. I admit I went out with Jack last night. And yes, we did kiss. But I didn't know he was still your boyfriend. He told me that you guys had split up.

Diane: Oh, come on, Karen. You can do better than that.

Karen: No, honestly, Diane, that's the truth. I wouldn't lie to you about something like this. Jack phoned me yesterday afternoon. He said he'd been wanting to go out with me for months. He told me he'd talked to you about his feelings for me, and you'd got angry and dumped him.

Diane: And you believed him, right?

Karen: Of course I wanted to check with you first. I tried to call you straight away, but your phone was switched off all afternoon.

Diane: I had dance practice.

Karen: Right, so you see... Well, Jack was really pushing me to go out with him. And to be honest, I've liked him for ages. But I'd never have gone with him if I'd thought you two were still together. You've got to believe that.

Diane: Maybe I will. Maybe not though. But I want to hear what he has to say first.

Conversation 2

Jack: Hello.

Diane: Hello, darling. Feeling better today, are you?

Jack: Oh, hi babe. What do you mean?

Diane: Well, yesterday you said you were feeling really sick. You phoned to cancel our date, remember?

Jack: Yeah, right. Well, I stayed home last night, got a good night's sleep, so I'm feeling a bit better today, thanks.

Diane: Oh, that's good. Only I was worried you might not have got enough sleep last night. Someone saw you in town at about 10 o'clock. At the Burger Heaven. With Karen.

Jack: Really?... Oh yeah, that's right. Karen called me about eight o'clock, said she wanted to talk. Asked me to meet her at the Burger Heaven. So I said okay.

Diane: She asked you out? To talk?

Jack: Yeah.

Diane: So what about the kissing?

Jack: What kissing?

Diane: Someone saw you Jack. Kissing.

Jack: Well, that was Karen. She suddenly started saying how much she liked me, and then she started kissing me. It was really embarrassing.

Diane: So why did you tell me you stayed home last night?

Jack: I didn't think you'd understand if I told the full story.

Diane: Bye, Jack.

Listening Clinic 2

1.   I can't believe you anymore.
2.   What did you say?
3.   I'm going to check up on you.
4.   I have told you time and time again.
5.   Shall we talk about this?
6.   Come here.

Word Lists

▶Unit 1: **Good to see you again**

tell me about it	an expression which means I understand how you feel
how's it going?	an informal greeting with someone you know
to rush to do something	to do something as soon as possible
....	an expression which means *congratulations!* or *well done*!
....	a bad dream
....	to begin a new thing
it's been ages	....
it suits you	....
let's get you...	....
....	....
....	....
....	....

▶Unit 2: **I've lost my rucksack**

document	an official piece of paper
to delay	to do something later than planned
to attach	to join, to fasten
....	a stand where newpapers and magazines are sold
....	a metal fastener on a belt
....	opposite of private
to calm down	....
to wrap around	....

you can't miss it	....
....	....
....	....
....	....

⊡Unit 3: **I'd like you to meet my brother**

modest	not loud or boastful
to take no notice of	to not pay attention to
gorgeous	beautiful
....	someone with experience who shows you how to do things
....	after waiting for a long time
....	someone who helps you do a job
used to do something	....
to show someone around	....
to catch something	....
....	....
....	....
....	....

⊡Unit 4: **Final Call for Flight EA42**

lounge	a comfortable room to sit in
patron	customer
to remind	to help someone remember something
....	by itself, not with a person

....	going to
....	right away, at once
announcement	....
seat allocation	....
connecting flight	....
....	....
....	....
....	....

▶Unit 5: It's a great deal!

a wide range	a large selection
trial	a time when you can try a new product or service to see how it works
fed-up	feeling tired of something
....	can be depended on
....	thin in a good way
....	to take a very long time
to rub	....
installation	....
original	....
....	....
....	....
....	....

▶Unit 6: That's not good enough

conventioneer	a person going to a large meeting
shuttle	a bus, plane or train that goes between two places not far apart

to point out a mistake	to show where something is wrong
....	to ask for too much money, to not follow the rules
....	a way of going someplace
....	an answer to a problem
to work on something	....
stretch	....
firm (adj)	....
....	....
....	....
....	....

Unit 7: Did you see the paper?

disposable	used for a short time and then thrown away
to launch a product	to start selling a new thing
estimated	guessed at (using information)
....	to get money for work
....	an official paper in which two people agree to something
....	money people make each month
to reach a peak	....
bonus	....
impressive	....
....	....
....	....
....	....

to drill	to practice something again and again and again
to rob	to use force to take money
to let someone in	to allow someone to enter
....	things people do regularly
....	to put something under the ground
....	a small house, usually in the wilderness
security	....
suspicious	....
gang	....
....	....
....	....
....	....

to swell	to become bigger than usual
diaper	underwear for babies
rash	a red area on the skin
....	feeling pain easily
....	a pain after eating
....	a sign of a sickness
to clear up	....
itch	....
to put on a bit	....
....	....
....	....

Unit 10: Could you give me a hand?

to stay up	to not go to bed
to take someone out	to go on a date with someone
allowance	money parents regularly give to children
....	to not have enough of something
....	to fight with words
....	an expression which means do something more quickly
fair	....
violent	....
to refuse to do something	....
....	....
....	....
....	....

Unit 11: This is six o'clock news

election	an event where people choose politicians
disaster	when something very bad happens
unharmed	not hurt
....	a person who puts money into a business
....	far from a center
....	specific information
to rescue	....

recovery	....
relief worker	....
....	....
....	....
....	....

Unit 12: Can I take a message?

to be tied up	to be busy
property	something that is owned
to reach someone	to get in contact with someone
....	something you like is going to happen
....	must be done quickly
....	a customer
to get in	....
to be out on a job	....
to arrange a meeting	....
....	....
....	....
....	....

Unit 13: How do you work this?

to get rid of something	to throw something out
that was painless	an expression that means something was easy to do
don't speak too soon	an expression that means *wait until we see the results*

....	an informal expression that means *wait*
....	the correct side is facing upwards
....	to take something out of something
to dub	....
to flash	....
to get something to work	....
....	....
....	....
....	....

Unit 14: Things have changed

you can't talk	an expression that means the person you are talking to does the same (bad) thing
to be sick of	to be tired of
to knock down	to destroy a building
....	to say something is not good
....	going forward, getting better
....	not very interesting
what about you!	....
romantic	....
to get through	....
....	....
....	....
....	....

to get stuck	to be unable to move
annoyed	not happy about something
to split up	to stop dating your boyfriend/girlfriend
....	to stop a plan
....	not planned
....	making you feel uncomfortable
upset	....
to admit	....
to dump	....
....	....
....	....
....	....

Audio CD Tracks for Exercises